A SEASON IN THE SYCAMORES

A SEASON IN THE SYCAMORES

A Father's Journey Raising an Outdoor Child

STEVEN T. FRANCIS

Paperback ISBN: 979-8-9910149-0-8

E-Book ISBN: 979-8-9910149-1-5

36 Degrees North, LLC
Elizabethtown, KY

DEDICATION

For my son, Gavin. All I have ever had to give to you was love and outdoor adventures. So, I wrote a few of them down.

CONTENTS

CHAPTER ONE

THE DAMNDEST TREE

I should feel bad for this, I think. Hating something that can't hate me back. It's an inanimate object—living, but inanimate—that can't move, or think, or feel, or hate. It had no intention of causing me this anger and frustration. It had no intentions of anything. It just is. It simply exists. I shouldn't feel these emotions about a tree, but there they are, burning hot and stuck high in my chest. I think I would cut it down if I had a chainsaw with me. Okay, so maybe I don't hate it. I love nature, so perhaps frustration is a better word. I'm a father now and must learn to deal with these frustrations. There is no room for hate. Hating a tree is just a waste of energy. But this particular tree; not just this individual specimen, but this whole species of tree, has been in my way all season long.

***

Go round up one hundred people. One hundred random Americans, from different socio-economic backgrounds and any area of the country you prefer. Take these people and ask them to name their favorite tree. Out of one hundred people, about 80 will give you a blank stare and say, "I don't know." They probably couldn't name a single species of tree if their lives depended on it. Of the remaining 20, about 10 will say "palm trees." They will say this because they love the beach, and it's a generic and recognizable tree. They won't realize when they give this answer that there are many different types of palm trees. There's the date palm, coconut palm, sabal palm... and probably a hundred more that I don't know. And what they are picturing in their head is probably a palmetto.

Your remaining 10 people may know something about trees, and will give a variety of answers. You may get a couple who say maple. After all, its leaf is on the Canadian flag, it produces a sweet sap that is reduced to make pancake syrup, and its leaves turn a brilliant shade of orange in the fall. You may get a couple responses for oaks, especially from deer hunters who keep a close eye on the acorn crop every year (or "akerns", depending on which side of the river you were raised). Others might say cedar for the smell, or fir for the nostalgia of Christmas. Someone may name a fruit tree, like apple or cherry, for obvious reasons. But, out of 100 red-blooded Americans, exactly zero will say their favorite tree is the American sycamore.

Zero.

I can't prove any of this, of course. Perhaps I should try. The American Society of Consulting Arborists is unlikely to see the value in such a study. and the University of Tennessee's botany lab would probably laugh at the research proposal. A qualitative study of peoples' favorite trees is probably not very useful to the scientific community. I could try and leverage every ounce of my influence with the U.S. Forestry Service, which is exactly zero ounces.

I guess if I were really dedicated to the cause, I could conduct the study on my own. I could round up 100 random people myself and pose the question, then document the findings to prove my point, but I don't have time for that. Like I said, I'm a father now. Anyways, I've always been better at speculation than research. And when you go trying to prove a hypothesis, all too often you just muddy the waters and end up more confused than convicted. I suppose that's the point of good science, but in this case, my hypothetical survey will be best left to hypothetical results. No one's favorite tree is the sycamore.

But, why not? It is abundant and easily recognizable. It has peeling gray and white bark with large leaves that turn a pallid shade of green, and then yellow in the fall. It is an unassuming tree, provides no food and is not widely used for building materials. No one paints them in pictures, or writes poems about their beauty, or hangs deer stands close to them. They certainly don't plant them on their property for future generations to sit in their shade and enjoy. But it doesn't make a mess or offend most people in any way. It is mostly unremarkable. For the most part, the sycamore just goes overlooked and unnoticed. It is a non-player in peoples' lives. The sycamore minds its own business, and people pay it no mind. But not me. I see it. And I see it for the menace it really is.

The American sycamore has one infuriating trait that most people don't know about. Only a small and specific group of people could possibly know. Fisherman. Anglers. Specifically, fishermen who have bad casting aim, or any who have taught a child to fish. Those poor, generous, ambitious souls who have taken a child into mentorship. This group of people have had the most exposure to this supremely frustrating trait. This dark secret of the American sycamore.

The sycamore's branches and leaves are an absolute *magnet* for fishing line. Once either line or lure touches one of the sycamore's wretched branches, it is absolutely stuck. I can't explain what the tree's specific traits are that makes this true, only that it is. There is a stickiness to the leaves, almost like Velcro. They feel slightly abrasive to the touch. Perhaps it's the size and shape of the leaves. They are large and broad, with jagged points and angles. The limbs may contribute as well. They are stiff and crooked and have a lot of smaller branches and twigs. Whatever the reason, if a lure, hook, sinker, or line so much as grazes a sycamore branch—it is stuck for good. Somehow, as the line touches the limb, it increases in velocity and spins violently around the branches, winding into an impossible knot, wrapping itself around the Velcro leaves in the process. And no amount of skill or finesse is going to shake or pull that sucker free. If you get hung up in a persimmon limb, or a maple, or a dogwood, or an oak, you at least have a chance. You might be able to reel it back over the limb slowly, or pull or shake the line free. These trees are reasonable, and more likely to give you back what is rightfully yours.

Not the sycamore. It takes, and it takes, and it never returns.

Some fishermen might know this, but most probably do not. They most likely have never noticed the correlation between lost lures and tree species. Don't take my word for it. Go prove it to yourself! And you don't even have to risk losing a lure to do it. Go to any popular, public fishing spot. Especially if it's a spot where kids are likely to have fished. Stand on the bank, or on the bow of your boat, and look for sycamore trees with limbs that stretch out over the water. There, you will see it. Colorful lures and plastic worms. Neon yellow and orange foam bobbers.

Wads of fishing line wrapped around limbs. Free running ends of 4 lb test, dangling and swaying in the breeze. It will look like a Christmas tree, with ornaments of every color and tinsel shimmering in the branches. Christmas in July.

On a calm day, if you close your eyes and clear your mind, you can probably hear the whispering echoes of past profanities exclaimed here under the sycamore leaves; echoing laments of someone fishing there with a child in the past. *"Shits"* and *"damnits"* whispered under the breath of fathers. *"Sons of bitches"* muttered through the clenched teeth of uncles and grandfathers. They drift on the breeze like ghosts.

It is my voice you hear. Mine, and the poor down-trodden souls like mine. Those who have stood on creek banks and shorelines with a child and freed snags, over and over. Those who have tied on 15 or 20 hooks in a single day. Those who have untangled impossible knots wrapped around spinning reels and sycamore limbs over, and over, and over again. Those noble men, with worn out fingers and bleeding hands, who ran out of bobbers and still tried to let the kid drop-shot fish on the bottom—knowing the chances of getting hung up would increase exponentially. Those who have suffered, endured, and persevered. And those who have done so with smiles on their faces, never letting the child see the unimaginable frustration boiling within. Poor bastards, every one.

CHAPTER TWO

ROCK FLIPPING

"Most people are *on* the world, not *in* it—have no conscious sympathy or relationship to anything about them—undiffused, separate, and rigidly alone like marbles of polished stone, touching but separate."
— John Muir, *The Unpublished Journals of John Muir*, 1938

Being an avid outdoorsman means having little choice but to become a sort of practicing naturalist. I have become a student of nature and my environment in this way. I'm not talking about tree worship or any of that hippie stuff. I have become a close observer of the natural world, but I have done so in order to become a more efficient predator. A better hunter, angler, and forager. A naturalist with a purpose.

I was lucky to have been raised as a hunter from a very young age. By both nature and nurture, I have come to devote my life to such pursuits as well as to fully understanding that this is the exception and not the rule in our modern world. Not rare enough to be considered unique, but not common enough to be commonplace. There are thousands of us, hundreds of thousands. We who, whether innate or learned, possess a burning desire to be grounded and connected to the natural world. And not merely as observers, but active participants. Part of the circle of life. In an increasingly synthetic modern world, we search for the organic. We seek out wild places and wild experiences. Like John Muir, we recognize that most people do not share this connection to nature—existing *on* this world, rather than *in* it. While our numbers as outdoorsmen are many, our percentage of the modern population continues to decrease. We are a dying breed of man, and woman, who must strive to protect our way of life and ensure its continuity. The most pragmatic way to go about this is to teach our children.

Teaching a child to be an active participant in the outdoors can take on many different forms, depending on the teacher, the family, and the environment. This will be heavily influenced by the mentor's specialty. It may mean learning to hunt deer or turkey, or forage wild mushrooms. It may mean learning to fish. Or perhaps it is just hiking and camping, although these last two activities border on observation rather than participation.

Whatever the pursuit may be, time spent outdoors with children is time well spent. But it ain't all sunshine and rainbows. It is a lot of fun, but it can be damned frustrating at times, too. Like anything worth pursuing, it is a lot of work. It requires sacrifice, and patience, and resilience, and compassion, and more patience. It's a grind. A process. The goal is not just to provide a kid with a fun day outside. It is not a singular experience. Rather, the goal is to instill a life-long love for the outdoors, and a deeply rooted connection to nature that will endure for years and generations to come.

And it all starts with "rock flipping."

Children are easy to impress because they are ignorant. I say this not as an insult, and certainly not to imply any lack of intelligence or aptitude. Not as a generalization anyway. There are dumb kids as well as smart kids, just like there are dumb adults. Without knowing the individual child, I cannot draw that distinction. What I can assert is that they are all ignorant. All of them. They simply lack experience. Everything in this big blue and green world is new and fresh and interesting to them. From birth until around eight years of age, everything in the world carries with it a sense of wonder and excitement.

When my son was of this age, everything was an adventure. During these formative years, we became semi-professional rock flippers. Probably could've gone full pro—if it was an officially recognized sport, of course. Rock flipping is an important step in the evolution of an outdoor child's life and education. The activity or skill probably lies somewhere between catching lightning bugs and learning to fish for bluegills.

The term "rock flipping" requires no explanation to those who grew up in the outdoors, or those who are raising a child to love and appreciate nature. But, to edify those who may have been raised in the city and are looking for a better way for their own offspring, I will elaborate. Rock flipping is exactly what it sounds like. You take a kid out into the woods, or to a creek, or in the backyard, and you look for cool stuff. The coolest stuff can often be found lurking under rocks or logs or anything else that can be flipped over. Find a rock, flip it over, and check out what is hiding underneath. This activity is absorbingly interesting to kids. You'll find bugs, worms, beetles, salamanders, frogs, spiders, snakes, and crawdads just to name a few possibilities.

Rock flipping is just good, clean fun. Well, clean in the sense that it is a wholesome and innocent pursuit, not in the sense that it is clean. It is actually quite the opposite. I have brought my son home from these rock flipping excursions covered in mud, dirt, blood, and frog slime more often than I have brought him home clean. In fact, the cleaner you come out of a rock flipping excursion, the poorer you likely performed during the event. This is an important part of it though. Kids should be allowed to get dirty.

Today's children live in a sterilized world. They spend 99% of their time indoors. They use hand sanitizer. They wear masks to school, or they did for a period of a few years until recently. Thankfully now, in 2024, we are coming out of the madness a little bit. But moms still use Lysol on every surface in the house. We wash our hands constantly. Kids are sheltered and disconnected from the natural world. Instead of playing outside in the dirt, they are playing video games and scrolling social media. This is not meant to be a rant against technology or modern conveniences, but rather a defense of "dirty fun."

Rock flipping is a great way to start the journey of getting children outdoors and instilling a sense of wonder and curiosity that can last a lifetime. If done properly, it will be a gateway to many other outdoor pursuits, like fishing and hunting. Fishing usually follows pretty close behind rock flipping, and this is where the real work begins. And make no mistake, it is real work. Although magnificently rewarding, it is a lot of hard work. But it is vitally important work, and it takes a dedicated parent—biological, adopted, surrogate, or otherwise—to facilitate the process. To light the fire.

That's the goal. Perpetuation of an outdoor lifestyle and protection of the places in which we live it. Like any dying culture, the best chance of preserving it is passing it on to our children. In fact, it is our only hope. This is how we keep the flame burning. We use it to light more fires. And when these children are grown, with children of their own, they will do the same. In this way, the flame of natural wonder, and our lifestyle, will endure for generations to come. If that doesn't work, nothing will. And to paraphrase a line from Robert Peck, I will stay until the fire dies. So it does not have to die alone.

Long after my bones have returned to the earth and been forgotten, I pray that my great great grandchildren will still be hunting the same mountains and fishing the same rivers I did. God willing, I will die on one of those mountains when I am an old man – old, but still healthy enough to be climbing mountains. Capable enough to climb, but too feeble to leave. Hopefully I'll have enough juice to get up there one last time, chasing a faint and distant turkey gobble or following a fresh set of deer tracks, when God sees fit to call me home. I hope the mountain is beautiful and wild and remote. I hope that my body is never found, so that my bones can stay there, against the base of some ancient oak tree with a rusted shotgun lying across both femurs of my lost and contented skeleton. And if there is no room for me in Heaven, I hope my soul can stay there on the mountain, too.

CHAPTER THREE

AN UNUSUAL DUCK SEASON

The sun rose on a hazy October morning in 2007. The sunrise happens fast in this part of the world. The land is flat all the way to the horizon, and it seems to go from dark to daylight quickly, skipping the long drawn-out "gray light" phase of the dawn that occurs in the mountains of East Tennessee. It was warm and dry. "Too warm for duck hunting," I thought to myself. The smell of diesel and dust hung low in the air as I waited in the parking lot for my guide to arrive. We had agreed to meet here at 0700. I had arrived a full 30 minutes early, for two reasons. First, my guide was the kind of person I did not want to keep waiting. Second, I was excited. I had hardly slept the night before in anticipation of that morning's hunt, which I knew would likely be my only waterfowl hunt of the season. I had a very busy schedule, and duck hunting opportunities were scarce here.

As the sun began to crest over the horizon, I could hear gunfire in the distance, to the south. It was coming from an unusual location. I wondered why anyone would be shooting there. The shots were sporadic and sounded lazy. I adjusted the position of the rifle slung across my chest. The guide was bringing a shotgun for me to use, but of course I had to bring my rifle along also. As I waited, I tried to count how many game laws I was about to break. I had no hunting license or federal duck stamp. I was carrying a rifle with me to the blind, even though we would be using shotguns for the hunt. We were shooting lead shot, #6's. And we had no intention of limiting ourselves to a bag limit of six ducks.

I know this seems self-incriminating, but I am confident we were outside of any state game agency's jurisdiction. Perhaps we could be prosecuted under federal game laws on a technicality, but surely the statute of limitations has expired by now. Maybe I am wrong. I guess it is possible that, after admitting my crimes, federal game wardens from the U.S. Fish and Wildlife Service may kick in my door and arrest me. If they do, I will comply. I will pay my fines and serve whatever community service the judge deems appropriate. Game laws aside, I doubt that the country of Iraq has a formalized waterfowl season. Even if they do, in 2007, with the war in full swing, they had much bigger problems at hand.

I had seen ducks in several places since arriving "in-country" and fantasized frequently about hunting them, often using the ACOG on my rifle to get a closer look. I had often seen mallards on the Tigris River. There were teal, blue-wing and green-wing, in the irrigation canals that cut through the farmlands around the river. I had even seen large flocks of canvasbacks on the lake around one of Saddam Hussein's palaces in Baghdad, their white feathered backs reflecting the intense desert sunlight like mirrors.

I waited in front of my Battalion headquarters on the north side of Forward Operating Base Anaconda. FOB Anaconda—which would later be renamed as Joint Base Balad—

was located outside the city of Balad, Iraq, and was home to the largest airfield north of Baghdad. The airfield had been taken early in the invasion of 2003 and occupied by U.S. Forces ever since. It had two large retention ponds at the north end that my guide said always had ducks on them. The ducks flying to and from the ponds posed a risk to military aircraft using the runways and so were routinely culled to reduce numbers and mitigate the risk by a couple of animal control workers. These civilian contractors not only killed ducks, but a species of pigeon called Iranian wood pigeons which were the largest pigeons I had ever seen. Big damn pigeons. They also trapped rats, jackals, and jack rabbits that may be vectors for disease on the base. My guide had explained that he sometimes participated in these cull hunts for fun. He was afforded such privileges.

The side-by-side pulled up at 0715. I stood at attention and rendered a sharp salute. My guide responded with a lazy gesture that was half salute, half wave, but mostly neither. "Knock that shit off and get in," he said. "Yes Sir," I replied, and clambered into the back seat.

My guide was Brigadier General Rob Hartnell, an Air Force one-star that was the commanding officer of the unit that controlled the Balad airfield. BG Hartnell and I had met under unfortunate circumstances a few days earlier, at a memorial ceremony for a mutual friend and colleague who had been killed in an IED strike. That airman had been under his command, and was an agent of a special intelligence team who worked with local Iraqi sources who secretly provided information to the U.S. military. I had worked with the fallen agent on a few occasions to provide security for the source meetings with my platoon. Tragically, on a recent source meeting mission, his vehicle hit an anti-tank mine that had been placed in front of the building where the meeting was being held.

   The general and the fallen airman were both from Arkansas. He had mentioned they were both duck hunters in his remarks, and I felt compelled to introduce myself. He was very personable and approachable, for a general officer, and he was country as cornbread. After the ceremony, I said hello and explained my connection to the fallen airman and offered my condolences. We then had a brief conversation after about how unfortunate it was that important things like duck seasons had to be missed for such trivial things as wars. We talked hunting for just a couple minutes, then parted ways. To my surprise, his aide called my battalion headquarters the next day and asked if I wanted to go "duck shooting" with the general. I jumped at the opportunity.

   We made our way toward the airfield, down dusty brown roads, past dusty brown buildings, under a dusty brown sky. Everything in this damn country was brown. The general spent the ride talking on a cell phone to staff officers, receiving updates and issuing orders. His aide, the driver of the side-by-side, was a young captain whose name I don't recall. He drove without instructions through the security checkpoints, onto the airfield, and down the fence line toward the retention pond. As we approached the pond, a flock of six mallards jumped out of the tall grass and flew across, landing again near the opposite bank. The general, still talking on the phone, pointed to the birds as they flew. The captain parked the side-by-side on the road above the pond and turned it off while we waited for the general to finish his phone call about logistics and redeployment. He and his unit were scheduled to change command and return to the States in two weeks.

The pond was a large rectangle, probably 300 yards long and 100 wide, with a thick band of phragmites growing around the edges that were about 8 feet tall and obstructed the view of the water when you got too close. These pale green reeds stood out sharply against the brown surroundings. The water, where we could see it, was dark green with algae on the top, and smelled like sewage.

The general finished his call and handed the phone to his aide. "Let's kill some birds before somebody else calls." He handed me a Mossberg 500 12 Gauge and a box of shells, then pointed down the bank and began to issue instructions. "We'll spread out down this bank and shoot away from the runway. Go down there about 100 yards. The captain will drive around the lake and jump 'em up for us."

As I walked away, I heard the general loading his shot-gun behind me. When I got into position along the east bank, the side by side began driving around from the general's position. I watched as a pair of teal jumped from the reeds and crossed in front of the general, from left to right. He shot twice. The lead bird folded on the second shot. His shots caused several ducks to jump from different areas of the lake. I shifted my eyes, trying to watch all the birds at once; mostly singles and pairs flying low over the tops of the tall reeds. Hearing a mallard hen quacking, I turned to my right and saw her flying higher than the other ducks and coming straight overhead, at about 30 yards. I shoul-dered the shotgun and fired once. It was a clean shot and she was dead in the air, falling belly-up into the tall reeds. The general fired again, but I didn't look over. My eyes were fixed on a small flock of teal, crossing right to left. I fired 3 times, dropping one bird in the water. The ducks that jumped from the lake seemed reluctant to leave. They usually stayed low and just hopped from one part of the lake to another. I reloaded in between shots, try-ing to keep a full magazine of five shells in the un-plugged shotgun; another game law we would be breaking if we were back in the States. A pair of teal swooped down, from right to left, and flared up from the top of the reeds. I missed twice. I desperately wanted to drop a duck onto the bank so that I could retrieve it, but every bird we'd killed so far had fallen into the tall reeds in the water. Wading into that nasty soup to search through the reeds was not an option. I watched the general drop a single mallard into the reeds. As I looked up, I saw a pair of teal flying straight at me from over the lake. I only had time to fire once. I dropped one of the teal, which nearly hit me as it fell onto the bank just behind where I stood.

Finally, I was able to pick one up. It was a hen blue-wing teal. She was brown and drab, just like the brown and drab world she lived in, except for the pale blue speculum on her wings. Between the two of us, we probably killed ten or twelve ducks in a matter of twenty minutes. The only two birds we were able to retrieve were my teal, and the general's mallard drake that was in half-plumage.

We met back at the side-by-side. The general was all smiles, and seemed genuinely happy to share the experience with a fellow duck hunter so far from home. He took a picture of me holding my teal and we loaded up to head back to the main base. We stopped to let the general out at his building first so that he could tend to important general officer business. He reached into his pocket and pulled out a challenge coin with his unit insignia engraved on it. He shook my hand, transferring the coin to me and said,

"Good shootin', Steve! Good luck with the rest of your tour. Look me up if you're ever in Arkansas."

"Yes Sir."

The general took a few steps, then turned back. "And be safe. There's a goddamn war goin' on out there."

That was the beginning and end of my 2007 duck season—short-lived, but unique—and I am grateful for the experience. When a federal game warden or the Iraqi Consulate knocks on my door, I fully intend to blame the general.

CHAPTER 4

QUARTER LIFE CRISIS

Most young men live their lives in a state of perceived invincibility. They believe—with their whole naive hearts—that nothing can possibly hurt them, and take unnecessary risks at every turn. Throwing caution to the wind, they perform acts of momentous bravery and reckless stupidity. These two qualities are often difficult to distinguish. Usually, their actions are motivated by some desire to impress a girl or gain the respect of friends. Feckless and irresponsible, they are quick to take a dare. Quick to accept a challenge. Quick to tempt fate. Some young men take this belief to the extreme and exhibit thrill seeking behavior. They thrive on danger and adrenaline. They drive too fast. They may drink. They often smoke. They may commit minor misdemeanors. It is a terrible trait in teenage boys, who are often responsible for their parents' hair turning gray long before it should. Sometimes over the course of just a few short years of late adolescence and early manhood. It is a terrible trait in young adults in general who may put innocent bystanders at risk, as they fly through life with little awareness of how their behavior may affect those around them. They make their fathers lose sleep at night. They make their mothers worry and pray and cry. They make police watch them with a suspicious eye. They make terrible citizens of their communities. They make damn fine soldiers.

My experience was no different. I hesitate to admit this, for fear that my own son may read these words one day and know the truth. I pray, as all fathers do, that he is smarter than I was and that he makes much better choices. I want him to understand that all young men grow into maturity and look back on their younger selves with a degree of embarrassment and relief that they made it through their younger, dumber days alive. It's always easier to see these things in retrospect, with the wisdom of another decade or two of experience. But it's hard to see it through a young man's eyes.

Youth is wasted on the young.

My most dangerous thrill-seeking phase came immediately after my first combat tour in Iraq. "If I survived the war", I thought, "I must be invincible." I didn't consciously think this, but it seems my subconscious must have believed it. I look back now and shudder to think about my stupidity.

I remember my family coming to visit me in Savannah, Georgia, shortly after returning from Iraq. We went to the beach on Tybee Island for the day. It was summer, and the beach was crowded. I remember walking into the water and people splashing all around me. I started swimming away from the beach. Away from the crowd and the noise. And I just kept swimming. Faster and faster. I didn't realize at the time that my dad and brother were following behind me. I kept going and going, until I was so far from the beach that I couldn't hear the people. In fact, I could only see the beach when the gentle waves lifted me high enough to peer over the swells. I don't know how far we had gone, but it had to have been close to a mile. My dad and brother had followed and tried to get me to turn back, but I don't think I even heard them. Why did I need to swim out that far? I don't know. Maybe to get away from all the people. Maybe for the peace and quiet. Maybe just to feel the abyss below me.

It was quiet there, so far from the shore. Peaceful. Three specks in an endless sea. Just the sounds of the wave swells and our own breathing. Not too far from civilization, but far enough that it was easy to pretend we were alone in the world. Above the abyss, vulnerable and peaceful, we floated on our backs and rested until the silence was interrupted by the sound of helicopter rotors in the distance. I was aware of the sound getting closer and louder, but it sounded muffled as I floated on my back with my ears underwater. It was so peaceful, I think I might have fallen asleep there for a moment. With my eyes closed, I envisioned the helicopter sound. In my mind's eye, I saw a familiar sight; two AH-64 Apache gunships circling overhead. One staying low and tight, one circling high and wide. It was a comforting sight, air support flying over my patrol. They could see down the crowded city streets where I couldn't see. I could almost hear the crackle of the radio as the pilots called on my radio frequency, "Viper 4-2, requesting task and purpose." Comforting. The sound grew louder and louder, until it snapped me out of my semi-conscious dream and back to reality. I opened my eyes to see a Coast Guard helicopter hovering overhead. I could hear a voice blaring from a loudspeaker or a megaphone on the helicopter. We couldn't make out their words over the noise of the helicopter, but the message was clear that they wanted us to swim back closer to shore. Annoyed, I reluctantly began swimming slowly toward the shore while the helicopter flew up and down the beach and never left our sight. My brother and father were relieved. They later expressed how dangerous the situation was, and how uncomfortable they had been with our adventure. I never felt an ounce of fear.

This is just one small example of how I lived my life at the time. This is how most soldiers and many young men live. Care-free, fearless, invincible. It was a great, immortal existence.

Then I became a father.

Of course, this changed everything. Fatherhood has that effect. Suddenly, my life was imbued with new meaning and purpose. The previously benign world around me became much more treacherous and foreboding. The ocean seemed deeper, waves more powerful, mountains higher and steeper, rivers swifter, whiskey stronger, 90 MPH a whole lot faster, and war more dangerous.

My son was only two months old when I deployed with my unit on my second tour in Iraq. I spent the next year away from home. I never saw him crawl. I missed his first steps, first words, holidays, and his first birthday. My experience in this regard was not at all unique.

During the height of the War on Terror, from about 2003-2012, active duty soldiers could expect to be deployed on a year on/year off schedule—twelve months "downrange" and twelve months home—over and over again. During the twelve months at home, lots of babies are born. Most are born about nine or ten months into the twelve-month rotation back in the States. Hospital maternity wards on Army bases across the country were overwhelmed during these deployment cycles. Unfortunately, this meant a lot of brand-new fathers were deployed while they had brand new babies at home, leaving brand new mothers behind to single-handedly bear the burden of parenting.

My unit landed in Mosul in October. When I stepped off the plane, it felt like I had never left. The air was hot and dry. Everything was still brown—ground, buildings, and sky—and the smells were familiar. Dust and JP8. We spent the next few weeks learning the operating environment, and in some cases learning our new jobs. Upon arriving, I learned I was to be an advisor and liaison to the Iraqi Army. This was great news for me! An interesting and exciting job. I had left the States thinking I would be a "battle captain" working in the Battalion Tactical Operations Center, or TOC. I dreaded the idea of working in the TOC every day. I could already feel the cabin fever setting in. This new assignment would have me going out on missions 2-3 times a week, and working with the local Iraqi Army Divisions.

We spent weeks making contacts with local leaders. Iraqi generals and colonels. Division and brigade commanders in the Second and Third IA Divisions in Al Kindi in downtown Mosul, and Al Kisik to the west, out near the Syrian border. We conducted training with their soldiers and helped with logistics and maintenance issues. We coordinated and conducted joint patrols with the Iraqis. Compared to my previous tour in Baghdad, my time in Mosul was peaceful. We had not received any enemy contact on the patrols, and mortar or rocket attacks on the FOB were rare. These had been an almost daily occurrence earlier in the war.

Then one day, for no particular reason, I was overcome with a sense of dread. It came out of nowhere one morning, before a mission, like a dark cloud looming overhead. I was convinced we would take contact that day. I just felt like something bad was going to happen. During 15 months of combat in

Baghdad, and several months up to that point in Mosul, I had never felt this way. But now I started to feel like I might not make it home. It was an overwhelming sensation of dread and worry. I pushed the feeling aside and we conducted our mission. We were leaving the south gate of FOB Marez and driving about an hour west, to meet with a general in the Third Iraqi Army Division. I double checked intel reports. I asked for air support and got it. A pair of OH-58 Kiowa helicopters would fly with us and scout ahead. I checked route clearance schedules and chose the most recently cleared routes through the city. We were as safe as we could possibly be, but the feeling remained. I commanded the lead truck and watched everything and everyone with a suspicious eye. There was a constant lump in my throat. As we approached Yarmouk traffic circle, I held my breath, almost expecting to get hit by an IED.

Nothing.

Nothing happened the whole day. The mission went as smoothly as any I had ever been a part of. There was no enemy contact. Not even any traffic through the city. We arrived back at the FOB that afternoon, and I breathed a deep sigh of relief as I removed my body armor. I went to the debriefing in the TOC, soaked through with sweat, with nothing significant to report.

Later that evening, as I sat in my room, I realized that the feeling still hadn't lifted. I was already dreading the mission I had scheduled for the next day. The feeling remained, day after day. I spent two weeks convinced that I might not make it home. Two weeks holding my breath every time I went through Yarmouk traffic circle. It was the most stressful two weeks of my life. All I kept thinking was that my son would grow up without his father. That was the worst part. I could accept my own fate, but I was worried for my son. It was an overwhelming anxiety.

I could hardly sleep. I sat up at night, playing guitar softly so as to not disturb anyone else in the old Iraqi Army barracks building we were living in. I wrote songs, or more accurately – lyrics. I had attempted writing songs ever since I started playing guitar in high school, but I could never quite unlock the secret of getting the lyrics and music to agree with one another to complete the process. I had journals full of lyrics, but when I tried to put them to melodies, it always came out sounding like a Soundgarden or Hank Williams song, or whatever I was listening to at the time. I eventually gave up songwriting, trading poetry for prose.

I even wrote "the letter." The letter you're not supposed to write. The one that some soldiers will say is bad luck. But I wanted my son to have something from me, my words. Something tangible that he could hold and read. Not just dog tags and a picture. I tried to write advice for his life that lay ahead of him. It seemed silly. What words of wisdom could a 26-year-old who had never done many wise things possibly impart?

Still, I tried to tell him who I was and what was important to me. I told him how much I loved his mother and asked him to always look after her. I encouraged him to live a life he could be proud of, and to do what makes him happy. I told him how badly I wanted to teach him how to fish and hunt, and I talked about the mountains and rivers where I would have taken him. I asked him to watch as many sunrises as he could in his life, because a man only gets so many. But mostly, I told him that I loved him and that I was sorry I couldn't be there.

It was a dark time. It was as close to touching bottom as I had ever been. Not because of my impending fate, but because of the family I would be leaving behind.

Then, after two weeks of knowing and accepting my fate, the feeling disappeared. It didn't fade. It didn't drift away. It was just gone. Suddenly and completely. I snapped out of it. I crumpled up the letter and threw it in the trash. I put the song lyrics in the back of a journal. I slept through the night. And I kept grinding through the rest of the deployment. The weeks that I thought would be my last on Earth turned out to be some kind of quarter-life crisis, prompted by my newly acquired position as a father. It was such a glaring juxtaposition. The tender love I felt as a father far from home, and the hard and unfeeling world of combat. It was just so difficult to reconcile the two.

I couldn't wait to get home and get to know my son. I couldn't wait to watch him grow and become whatever it was he would eventually become. I couldn't wait to show him the mountains and rivers myself, and to teach him how to hunt and fish. I dreamed about showing him the vivid colors of a wild sunrise in the Tennessee mountains. Fatherhood would surely be the greatest adventure of all.

CHAPTER FIVE

WASTED SUNRISES

"Full many a gem of purest ray serene
The dark unfathom'd caves of ocean bear:
Full many a flower is born to blush unseen,
And waste its sweetness on the desert air."

—Thomas Gray, *Elegy Written in a Country Churchyard*, 1751

How many sunrises does the average person experience in their lifetime? Not through the windshield of a car on their way to work, or the window of a waiting room on the morning of an early doctor's appointment. How many do they truly experience, with all their senses?

There is a barrier that an office window or a car windshield emplaces that is stronger than the thinness and clarity of the glass may suggest. No matter how clean and transparent, a window can't let in the sunrise. The witness on one side of the glass is just a distant observer. A viewer. A distant spectator of an event occurring apart from them on the other side. To these witnesses; at least those with the presence of mind and awareness to even notice, this spectacular event may be extremely beautiful. But it is beautiful in the way that a painting is beautiful. Or a photograph. Or a touching scene at the end of a romantic movie. It is 2-dimensional. Shallow. Something gets lost in translation. It remains stuck there, on the other side of the windshield, with the yellow pine pollen and smears of bug guts.

Many of these witnesses may notice and appreciate the sunrise for a moment, but quickly become distracted. They notice and appreciate the beauty as an aside. On their way to something more important. Maybe they think about the job they are driving to, or their to-do list for the day. They listen to the scores of yesterday's football game on the radio, or the latest celebrity gossip, or the state of the latest war in whatever poor, far-off country that is warring at the time over oil or religion or ancestral lands. Distraction is the enemy of true and meaningful experience.

In the fast-paced world of today, it has become fashionable to be good at multitasking. It is even a point of pride for many people. They put the term on their resumes and use it in interviews. It's a buzz word that people think makes them seem intelligent and capable.

This is a dangerous notion. And it is a lie.

A person cannot fully devote themselves to more than one task at a time. At least, not if the task or activity at hand requires any level of thought or attention at all. Ask a fighter pilot. Or an infantryman. Or a nurse. Or a firefighter. Or a tax accountant. They know. You must be present and in the moment. The only task that matters is the current one. The current step on your checklist, or your pre-flight, or your battle drill. They know they must complete that task. Singularly. While completely present. And with their full attention. The same is true of sunrises.

To truly experience a sunrise, you have to bathe in it. You have to stand in the open air, under the sky, and let the light flow over your skin. You have to breathe it in deep and hold it in your lungs. You have to wait on it and let it open up to you. You must surrender to it and give it your full attention. Unfiltered and unobstructed. Without distraction or interference. How often do people experience this spectacular event to the fullest? How many have never really experienced it at all? It happens every day, yet most don't bother to notice, and they go through life never realizing how much poorer they are for it. Like Thomas Gray's flower and the desert air – the sweetness is wasted.

Hunters and anglers are fortunate, by the nature of their avocation, to witness more sunrises than probably any other group of people, except for maybe insomniacs and third shift workers. They will also, almost invariably, see them through much less obstruction and distraction, and with much more hope and gratitude. This is one of the traits of the outdoors lifestyle that keep outdoorsmen and outdoorswomen coming back for more. The sunrise, and the day that it belongs to, holds the promise of adventure and the mystique of the unknown. A wild and mysterious type of beauty that can rarely be rivaled by anything else in life. Rarely have I felt more alive than when standing on top of a mountain, alone, watching the world wake up as the morning sun shines her light across a wild landscape, bathing it in a renewed sense of purpose and hope.

We only get so many. I try not to waste them.

CHAPTER SIX

THE BOY ON THE RIVERBANK

The boy was five years old the first time he saw it. He didn't know what he was seeing at the time, but the father did. The boy was five years old because the mother would have it no other way. This was the minimum age. It had been pre-determined before the boy's birth. The timing and details of this day had been fiercely debated by the parents, years in advance of this morning. The mother won, as mothers usually do, and the agreed upon age was five years old. The boy would be five years of age before the father was allowed to take him on his first real hunting trip.

The father—had he been allowed to carry out his reckless and irresponsible plan, would have taken the newborn straight from the hospital, swaddled him in a camouflage blanket, or perhaps burlap, filled a thermos of lukewarm baby formula, and put him in a duck boat to go hunting. The necessary precautions that would be required for newborn babies going duck hunting would have been taken, of course.

The child would have been dressed in warm clothes and required to wear hearing protection. He would have been fitted with some form of floatation device, as required by Tennessee state law. As safely as possible, the boy would have been introduced to the world on his first day of life—before God and all His creation, in the wild. Baptized in cold air, sunshine, and the promise of adventure. This hypothetical scenario is slightly exaggerated, of course, but only slightly.

The reality is that cooler heads and maternal instinct prevailed. The baby boy was swaddled in one of those standard hospital baby blankets. The one with the teal and red stripes that every hospital has used since at least the 1960s. He drank his formula from a bottle instead of a green Stanley thermos. No hearing protection or floatation device was required to be worn for several years, because he was never in a situation that threatened neither hearing damage nor boating accidents. And he was introduced to the world in the same normal, boring way all other babies are introduced. Family visits and mailed cards and texted pictures. And the child's first 1,800 or so sunrises were witnessed through the windows of houses, cars, and daycare facilities.

But on the opening day of duck season, in the boy's fifth year of life, he witnessed his first wild sunrise. It was an unseasonably cold November morning for East Tennessee. There was a heavy frost on the ground when the father woke his son. Preparations had begun hours earlier. The boy's grandfather and uncle had been busy on the riverbank, doing their part to ensure the success of the event. They had agreed to arrive a full two hours before sunrise to secure the spot and shine off any other hunters that may come in by boat. To occupy their time before the little boy's arrival, they built a massive blind out of dead grass and cattails. They brought folding chairs and laid scrap plywood on the ground in the blind, to make it a little less muddy, as well as a small propane heater which they nestled into the corner. The boy, his father, and mother would be there much closer to sunrise to limit the boy's exposure to the harsh weather and keep him from getting bored waiting for daylight. This was a family event that everyone wanted to be a part of.

The place itself was very special. It was not special in the sense that it was a good hunting spot. Quite the opposite, actually. Of all the times the family had hunted this spot, they had gone home empty handed much more often than not. But still, occasionally there was a flock of geese that would fly along the west bank of the river. Ahead of a cold front, there were usually a few mallards that could be seen flying high against the backdrop of the mountain. And there was always a possibility of wood ducks which spent most of the year in the area because it rarely got cold enough so far south to force them to migrate. This place was not special because it was any sort of waterfowl haven. But it was a beautiful place, with easy access to walk to the river for the boy's first hunt.

The spot in question is up-river from the Alabama state line and down-river from Chickamauga Lake, on the Tennessee River, which narrows down the description to about 30 linear miles of riverbank. And that is about as precise a location as you could ever hope to get from a duck hunter talking about a hunting spot – even if it's not a good one.

The father would come here often during duck season, and sometimes when it was not duck season. He came here when he needed to be alone, or to feel grounded. He had come here when he was home on R&R from the war and couldn't sleep. He came hours before sunrise and filled his lungs with the cold February air. He sat on the banks and prayed and worried for his friends back in Baghdad. He drank coffee and watched the sunrise and tried to calm his restless soul.

At this point in its journey from the Appalachian Mountains to the Mississippi, the Tennessee River is about a quarter mile wide, as it winds between large, steep mountains. Sunrises here are unique in that you will not feel the direct rays of the sun until two hours after sunrise. The mountains tower above in every direction, so the sun will not crest over the peaks and shine down into the narrow river valley until after 9am. In the valley between the mountains, you witness a sort of indirect sunrise. You don't see the sun's light and feel its warmth as it crests over the distant horizon; instead, the world lights up slowly in the shadow of the mountains. The fog lingers on the water, as the sky begins to glow and reveals the silhouette of the ancient cliff lines across the river. The ambient color from the sunrise on the other side of the mountain spills over the cliffs and pours into the river valley in a cascade of glowing orange. Color from the sunrise that you can't see fills the valley from the bottom, up. The fog on the water turns to fire and the very air in the valley turns golden. On a particularly cold morning, when the fog is thick and your breath hangs in front of your face, the temperature actually drops a degree or two at sunrise. Despite it being a sunrise you can't actually see, it warms your soul from the inside out with the promise of heat and energy that will soon flood the valley.

The boy's first adventure was on just such a morning. The father, the boy, and the mother arrived just before shooting light. They parked the truck on the side of the mountain road and began to prepare – putting on the final layers of clothing, rounding up lost gloves and toboggans, and gathering essential supplies from the back seat. The boy was dressed in so many layers he could barely move, and his walk looked clumsy. The mother grabbed the thermos of hot chocolate from the floorboard. The father carried an old, professional looking shotgun with worn bluing on the receiver and a wooden stock that looked like it had been chewed by a beaver.

The young family made their way through the woods in the gray light of the morning towards the riverbank. The boy stumbled and fell multiple times along the way. He carried a flashlight and shined it around erratically as he climbed over logs and stepped over ruts in the ground. It was a short, 300-yard walk to the river where the boy's uncle and grandfather were waiting in the blind they had built for the morning. The father tried to hurry the boy along. It was already legal shooting light, and he could hear the whistle of wings and wood ducks squealing overhead. The father was surprised he hadn't heard any shots ring out from the blind yet. The young family arrived and got the boy into the blind. He sat in a folding chair, and the mother secured his hearing protection firmly over his ears. Hot chocolate was poured from the old green thermos and the boy eagerly grabbed the cup.

The father heard the whistle of wings and knelt next to the boy and directed him to look up at the sky. A pair of wood ducks circled wide overhead, squealing through the morning air. The boy watched as the ducks came back around, aiming to land in the beaver swamp behind the blind. The uncle shouldered his gun and made a beautiful shot as the ducks passed from right to left. The drake folded and splashed in the swamp behind the blind. The grandfather didn't shoot – he was too busy watching the boy. The father never even loaded his gun. The uncle retrieved the bird and handed it to the father, who then presented it to the boy. It was a flawless drake wood duck that didn't have a noticeable scratch on it, and looked like it could come back to life and fly away at any second.

The boy was amazed by the colors. He removed his glove to feel the feathers, and gasped when he ran his hand over the soft down feathers underneath. "It's warm!" he said. He sat and admired the colors. The father turned the bird slightly, showing the boy the iridescence in the feathers and how they change colors when viewed from different angles. Subdued hues of copper, blue, and green overlaid against a black canvas. The boy was fascinated by the vermiculated feathers on the duck's sides, golden and black. He pulled down the eyelids and looked at the red eyes. He ran his fingers against the grain of the fine, hair-like feathers on the duck's head.

As the glow of the sun rolled over the mountains and began to ignite the river fog in a glow of orange, the father answered a slew of questions from the boy. He watched the boy admire the duck, and sat with him on the riverbank to dangle his feet in the water and splash with his boots. The father imagined what it must be like for the boy to be experiencing these colors, smells, and sounds for the first time. He wondered what it all looked like through a child's eyes. Innocent eyes. Eyes that have never seen violence and war. He wondered what the morning air smelled and tasted like through a child's senses, before they had been dulled for years by tobacco and whiskey.

He guessed the morning air probably tasted sweet to the boy. The father couldn't help but feel a little jealous. He wondered what it was like to experience the wonder of the wild world for the first time. Then, as he was watching the boy, he realized he didn't have to wonder. He was experiencing it all for the first time all over again through the child. This is the privilege of fatherhood. And suddenly, he too could taste the sweetness of the morning air.

CHAPTER SEVEN

PATIENCE

Merriam-Webster defines "patience" as "*the capacity, habit, or fact of being patient.*" This, in my opinion, is a terrible definition because it uses the root of the defined word as its definition. Webster then defines the word "patient" as "*bearing pains or trials calmly or without complaint.*" There are two distinct parts to this definition. First, "*bearing pains or trials.*" This happens to everyone, to some degree. There is a Buddhist saying, "Existence is suffering." We all suffer. While some endure far more pain and suffering than others, but we all experience it. Such is life. The second part of the definition, "*calmly or without complaint*" is where things start to get interesting. This is what separates the sinners from the saints.

We all suffer, but most of us do so with a significant amount of complaint. It's human nature. We want others to recognize our pain and suffering. Now, that's not to say that the man who complains about their suffering is inherently bad, or less virtuous than the man who suffers in silence. There are people who endure a hell of a lot of trials and tribulations and keep on going. They endure. They work hard. They get the job done, no matter what! And they bitch and moan and grumble and complain the whole time. They absolutely deserve our respect. But, this is not patience. This could maybe better be defined as resilience. Everyone has heard the phrase, "Patience is a virtue." Well, so is resilience.

Over the course of my life, I have been involved in endeavors that require a great deal of resilience. I have taught middle school history in the public school system. I have led soldiers in combat. I have led soldiers in garrison. I draw a distinction between combat leadership and garrison leadership deliberately, because the dynamic is so incredibly different. In many ways, it requires more resilience to manage a squad or platoon or company of soldiers in garrison than it does in a combat zone. This may come as a surprise to civilians, but it's true. If you don't believe me, go and find a veteran who held any position of leadership—from fire team leader all the way up to brigade commander—and ask them. I am confident their answer will track.

Soldiers who joined the military from 2001 to about 2014 did so with the full understanding that they were going to war. We call veterans of this era GWOT veterans, or Global War On Terrorism. While most of those years did not see the same intensity of conflict as Vietnam, Korea, or WWII, they resulted in periods of intense combat and long periods of sustained combat operations. The men and women who joined the military during this time joined to fight. While deployed, they were focused. They understood their role in the greater mission. They conducted themselves with professionalism and fought with honor and valor. They woke up in the morning with purpose and worked together toward a common goal. There were exceptions, of course… there's a bad apple in every bushel, but generally speaking, these were great young men and women. America's finest.

Then, the deployment ends and they go home.

Garrison Army service offers a completely different set of challenges compared to war-time Army. The young soldiers, who just weeks before fought honorably and valiantly, now find themselves overwhelmed. Sometimes the re-deployment can be too much. Everything is too much. Too much freedom. Too many choices. Too much time. Too much energy, aggression, testosterone, and an unmet need for action or adventure.

Not enough purpose. Not enough outlets for the emotions and hormones. "*Idle hands and the devil...*" or however that Bible verse goes.

So, with all this pent-up energy and aggression, naturally, they get into trouble. They drink too much. They get into fights. They have domestic problems. They get arrested. They experiment with drugs. They sneak girls, or groups of girls, into the barracks with less than honorable intentions. They spend all of their money, and then they spend some more money. And then they go take out payday advance loans, with 30% interest rates, and spend even more money.

The poor bastards responsible for these young soldiers— the Leaders, spend a large amount of their time cleaning up the ensuing mess. First sergeants and sergeants major spend innumerable hours on counseling, bailing 19–22-year-old kids out of jail, chasing down child support payments for estranged spouses, and more counseling. Battalion commanders and company commanders hold courts martial, and article 15's, and track down AWOL soldiers. And every one of them, from the rank of staff sergeant to general, wishes for just one thing.

They wish to go back to combat. They want to go back to where things were simpler. Where everyone had a job – a purpose.

All of this requires a leader to have great resilience. You must endure a lot of hardship. But the one advantage that an Army captain has over a new father, is that the captain can complain. He need not suffer in silence. However, he must exercise tact and good judgment when voicing his frustrations. Complaints generally go up the chain of command, not down. And good leaders generally get a lot more done with conversation than with yelling. But, sometimes an army leader just has to look a soldier in the face in their moment of trepidation and say "That's the stupidest damn thing I've ever seen. Pull yourself together!"

A young father has no such luxury. He cannot complain in the same way the sergeant or the captain can. He must suffer in silence. He must deliver corrections and instructions for the $1,000^{th}$ time, in calm tones, and with a smile on his face. He must be patient. Truly patient. Having been both the Captain and the young father, I can say categorically that having patience—true patience—is infinitely harder than merely being resilient. There are many ways to learn and practice resilience. A great example is military service, as we just discussed, but also team sports, learning a trade, higher education, going into business, and the list goes on.

There are also many ways people may attempt to learn true patience. A monk may meditate on a mountaintop for years. A woman may plant and tend to a garden, waiting for weeks to see the fruits of her labor. A man may invest in a start-up company and wait years to see if his investment matures. You can practice mindfulness, as my therapist calls it, which is a new buzzword in mental health circles... whatever the hell that means. He tried to explain it to me, but it's one of those abstract and obscure things that no one can really explain very well— like déjà vu. Or infinity. Or gluten.

Whatever path to patience or enlightenment that one may choose to pursue, there is one endeavor that rises above all others in difficulty, but also in efficacy. It is a treacherous road, littered with obstacles and challenges and un-imaginable frustrations. It is a roller coaster of emotions that will test even the strongest of wills. Forget going to seminary, or meditation, or yoga, or vows of silence, or practicing a life of celibacy. Want to achieve true patience, of the highest level any man can achieve in this life? I can tell you how.

First, become a parent. You can do this by whatever means you feel is appropriate. The traditional way, adoption, surrogacy, or otherwise. Second, see to it that the child becomes curious about the outdoors and the natural world. And finally, when the child is of an appropriate age (more on this later), teach the child to fish. This should not be confused with, "Take the child fishing" which implies a single event. Spend whatever time is necessary to teach the child HOW to fish. Within this simple sounding task resides a multitude of implied tasks. This will take time. How much time, I cannot say. My data set is too small to attempt to draw an educated conclusion. I have only produced the one child, and therefore have only attempted the teaching process one time.

One time was enough.

CHAPTER EIGHT

NEGLIGENT DISCHARGE

The term "accidental discharge" was a term used in the U.S. Military for ages and describes an accident involving a weapon where the operator fires a round when he does not mean to. This presents many problems, as one might imagine. First, and most obviously, it is a severe safety hazard. Second, it is unprofessional. And third, it is damn embarrassing for the offending party. As it should be. Any person, soldier or civilian, who is in possession of a firearm should be in complete control at all times. All actions performed with a weapon, or while in possession of one, should be performed deliberately and with the utmost care and caution. Failure to do so endangers every person, friend and foe, in the immediate vicinity. In a combat zone, it is imperative that everyone maintains the highest standards of weapons discipline. Failure in this regard endangers the lives of everyone in the vicinity. The weapon is only a machine. It can make no distinction between enemy and friend.

Fratricide is the worst of all the "cides."

At some point in the early 2000's, back when the nation settled into a period of long and steady combat operations in the

Middle East, the U.S. Army transformed from a peace-time force to a professional, war-time force that became accustomed to conducting sustained combat operations on a regular cycle. It was during this time when the term "accidental discharge" transitioned to "negligent discharge."

The word "accidental" carries with it a light-hearted "oops, my bad" sort of connotation, whereas "negligent" is much more assertive. Negligence implies culpability. That the offending party was in control of his actions the whole time and still committed the offense. In pulling the trigger, he probably did not mean to harm anyone, but he failed to control his body and his weapon—which is an extension of his body. In a war-time Army, such negligence cannot be tolerated. Negligent discharges are dealt with swiftly and firmly, as they should be. Most cases usually involve some level of recourse from the Uniform Code of Military Justice (UCMJ). Others may only result in a little "motorpool justice" which is far less formal, but painful and humiliating in its own way. Which version of punishment is administered depends largely on who was present to witness the crime.

Two personal stories come to mind, from two consecutive summers in Iraq. The names of the characters have been changed to protect the not-so-innocent.

In the Summer of 2007, in the small town of Al Jamiya, Iraq, my unit was conducting a presence patrol. The patrol consisted of three HMMWVs, and its purpose—as you may surmise—was to show presence outside of the Forward Operating Base. This was a deterrent strategy. During the course of the patrol, we were ordered by the Battalion HQ to detain a man for questioning. The man was actually an informant who we were to publicly detain and bring to the base and make it look like it was against his will to any insurgents that may be watching. As an Iraqi civilian, with terrorists in your village, the last thing you want is for the bad guys to think you are cooperating with the Americans. While detaining this man, he was searched for weapons and documentation. The soldier searching the man, Specialist Cooper, found a pistol in the waistband of the Iraqi man's pants. It was a rusty, semi-auto 9mm, probably Czech or Yugoslavian, that looked like it would take half a can of WD-40 to even get the safety off. Apparently, the safety was already off. SPC Cooper took the pistol with his right hand, placed his left hand on top of the slide with both elbows out, and pushed against the slide in order to open the chamber and clear the weapon. His negligence was in where he was pointing the gun, and where both of his hands were placed. His right index finger was on the trigger, and the meaty part of the outside of his left hand, next to the pinky, was over the end of the barrel. The weapon fired and the bullet went completely through his hand. A neat, clean 9mm hole and a broken metatarsal bone below the pinky. Of course, there was no hiding this incident. SPC Cooper had to go to the hospital for medical attention, and cleanly blown holes through a soldier's hand tend to raise questions. The incident was reported through proper channels. As if his non-combat related injury and the humiliation weren't punishment enough, SPC Cooper received an Article 15, and promptly became Private First Class Cooper.

About one year later, in the Summer of 2008, the 2nd Brigade of the 3rd Infantry Division was in its 13th month of a 15 month deployment. My unit, a security platoon, was stopped on Route Jackson, just south of Baghdad. We were in the process of recovering an armored vehicle that had broken down in the road. It was at least 110 degrees, probably 120 on the pavement between all of the vehicles. Traffic was held up in every direction, and the situation was growing more tense by the minute. Everyone was hot, tired, hungry, pissed off, and on edge. That is when mistakes tend to happen.

When the shot rang out, everyone who was dismounted from the vehicles ducked and crouched next to cover. Everyone except Private Castillo. Private Castillo just stood there, in front of God and everybody, looking pale as a ghost. Drops of sweat fell from his nose in a steady rhythm, like a leaky faucet, as he stared down at the fresh bullet hole in the pavement next to his left foot. The gunners in the HMMWVs and the dismounts on the street scanned the buildings and traffic for threats. Then everyone began to realize what had happened. As the platoon leader, I already dreaded submitting the incident report and writing sworn statements. Then I realized, no one was hurt, nothing had been called in on the radio, and I was the highest-ranking leader on the ground. As if he had realized it at the same time, my platoon sergeant looked at me and said, "I got it, Sir. Call it in as a warning shot." Warning shots happen all the time. They are a required part of escalation of force, when time permits, to avoid using lethal force except when necessary.

I don't know what variety of "motorpool justice" was administered to Private Castillo when we got back to the FOB. I do know that my platoon sergeant was a good leader, and no one harmed Private Castillo in any way. He likely enjoyed some rigorous physical training, and maybe a little humiliation to atone for his sins. No UCMJ action needed, and everyone could focus on the next day's mission.

There is another kind of negligence that I discovered many years later. Like the negligent discharge, it also involves a projectile of sorts, a certain amount of danger, and even more frustration. However, this negligence doesn't result in a discharge, but rather, the lack of one. A negligent non-discharge. The danger is not quite as grave, but the level of frustration it elicits is enormous. The subject of the negligence and the frustration is a seven-year-old boy and a spinning reel.

When it comes to operating fishing equipment, a rod and spinning reel is about as simple and versatile as it gets. There are several other options available. Bait casters are a little more advanced, and generally used by serious bass anglers. Fly rods require a level of finesse, and pretentiousness, that most mortal men will never achieve. Most of us stick to spinners. Most everyone knows how to operate this essential tool, but to edify those who may have never been fishing, or those rich kids who grew up fly-fishing trout streams and think there is no other acceptable method, I will take a brief moment to explain its operation. Spinning reels spin using a gear ratio that allows smooth release and retrieval of the fishing line. There is a mechanism on the reel called a bell that must be opened—or "flipped"—to allow the line to pull out of the reel freely. Once the bell is closed, the line can then be wound back into the reel. You open the bell to cast, and you close it to reel. Simple, effective, and generally very user-friendly. That is, unless the user is a brand-new fisherman—age 7.

The sun rose on a humid late-July morning in Middle Tennessee. It was getting hot already and the air seemed stagnant. The water in the lake seemed stagnant, too. We left the boat at home, opting to target a spillway where the flowing water from the impoundment into the river would provide more oxygenated water and concentrate the fish. The spillway was not a dam, just a simple culvert under the gravel road from the impoundment into the Cumberland River that lets excess water flow out to maintain a constant water level in the lake.

We parked the truck on the side of the gravel road and walked down to the mouth of the spillway with our gear. I carried two fishing rods. I always carried two fishing rods. Not because there would ever really be two people fishing, but because I knew we would need a back-up. As we made our way down the bank, I looked up into the branches of the sycamores over the water and briefly considered how someone could come here with a pole saw and retrieve a hell of a lot of lures and bobbers from the trees. We reached the water's edge and set our gear down; two rods, a small tackle box, a cooler containing a can of red worms, and a bag of snacks. The boy looked at the water eagerly. As always, I took the opportunity to put a fresh pinch of Copenhagen in my lip with my clean fingers before the dirty work began. Not that I mind the taste of worm and bluegill with my Copenhagen too much, it's just a different flavor pairing that I would get on my next dip about an hour later. I took a worm out of the can and baited a hook.

The boy's first cast was beautiful. I was filled with a sense of pride watching his smooth and gentle side-arm cast, 20 feet out and slightly to the right. The bait landed in the slack water, just outside the edge of the swift flowing water of the spillway. He closed the bell of his reel and almost instantly his bobber disappeared. The tip of his five foot rod bent over and the fish began running hard, from left to right. The boy exclaimed, "It's a good one!" He fought the fish and pulled it away from the log it was aiming for, slinging it out of the water and into my lap. It was a large redear sunfish, or "shellcracker" as they are called in this part of the country. We admired its dark back and fins, green speckled sides, and reddish-orange gill flap that gives it its name. We put the fish on ice and re-baited the hook. We were off to a good start.

The boy took aim at the same spot at the edge of the swift water, held the rod back and made the same smooth casting motion as before. Only this time, the bait did not splash. The hook and sinker recoiled back and twirled around the end of the rod. The line seemed to accelerate as the free-running end got shorter. The bobber somehow spun around the rod, in the opposite direction as the hook and sinker, and worked the whole line into a formidable Gordian's knot. The boy realized instantly what had happened. He forgot to flip the bell. Three feet of line had whipped around at the end of his enthusiastic cast.

Negligence.

"It's okay buddy, use this one." I handed him the back-up rod, already baited with a fresh worm. While I began trying to untangle the knot, the boy made another good cast and instantly hooked into another fish. He reeled in a beautiful bluegill. I told him to hold on a second as I finished untangling the knot. It's times like these when I wish I had three hands. He made a few more good casts and landed a couple more bluegill. I stood beside my son, baiting hooks and unhooking fish, and absolutely soaked in the moment. I breathed deep and watched the action. I smiled and soaked up the morning sun flickering through the trees to our left. I absolutely wallowed in it. I started to think I might be able to get a cast or two in myself.

About that time, the boy got hung up on something out in the water. I whipped the rod up and down and tried to get it free, but it wouldn't budge. I pulled and broke the line. Handing the boy the back-up rod, I sat down and began tying the hook on the broken line. I saw the boy make a casting motion out of the corner of my eye, and then jerk around toward me. I looked up to see the nest of line around the tip of the rod. Another negligent non-discharge.

"You gotta remember to flip the bell, bud!" I said calmly, trying not to let any frustration cut into my tone. The boy apologized. Handing him the rod I had just finished tying, I knelt down behind him and began the de-tangling process all over again. The boy made a couple casts and put a fish in the cooler by himself. He baited a hook, and I complimented him on his self-sufficiency. I was glad he was in the zone, because I was knee deep in this knot. I had line in both hands, and some between my teeth, separating parts of the knot with different fingers. Intensely focused on the task at hand.

They say in moments of fear or moments fueled by adrenaline that time slows down. You see it in war movies sometimes; a shell-shocked soldier on the beach in Normandy, looking around as explosions launch sand into the air in slow motion, and people scramble for cover. A terrified radio operator lying against a berm in a rice paddy in Vietnam, with bullets cracking overhead and his platoon sergeant yelling instructions in slow motion. Thankfully, I never experienced this phenomenon in my war, even during my most intense experiences.

But as I worked on this knot, with fingers and teeth holding line, and my hands up close to my face, time slowed down. I remember, in exquisite detail, watching a worm land on the back of my left hand. It was only inches from my face. I saw the specks of moist, black soil still on his body. I watched, for what seemed like a full two seconds, as the worm wiggled slightly on the back of my hand. We looked at each other, eye to eye—if worms had eyes—and both accepted our fate. I saw the shimmer of the hook, and had a brief moment to admire the perfect knot tied on the eyelet. "Damn, I tie a good knot. I have definitely had plenty of practice today." Simultaneously, I noticed the form and motion of my beloved son, about six feet beyond the worm on my hand, and out of focus. A blurry form in the stance of mid-cast and about to sling the rod forward and possibly drive the hook into my hand. Time stood still, but so did my body. As he launched the rod forward to finish the cast, time's march fell back into normal cadence. I snapped back to reality. I braced for impact, and felt the tip of the hook lodge into the back of my hand.

There is no "cide" like fratricide.

Luckily, the boy had flipped the bell open this time, and as he casted forward, he was releasing the pressure on the line from his finger. This meant there was only minimum forward motion of the hook, and only the tip penetrated my hand. No real harm done. I wiped the speck of blood on my pants and told my son that the blood on the hook will just chum the water and make the fishing better. Though I warned him that it might attract sharks, so he shouldn't fall in the water. He laughed.

This cycle of catching fish and untangling knots continued for another hour or so, until the boy got tired and hungry. We made our way back up the bank, to the truck parked on the gravel road. Exhausted and dirty and bloodied and happy. With a cooler full of bluegills to fry for dinner. The boy was asleep in the back seat before we even made it back to the highway.

CHAPTER NINE

REQUIEM FOR A CROW

Perhaps the greatest responsibility of a parent raising a child to be a hunter is imparting proper morals and ethics to the child. In almost all cases this part of the child's education occurs naturally and through close observation of the parent. Direct instruction is rarely needed. This is usually a good thing; that is if the parent conducts themselves in a legal and ethical manner. But like any other facet of life, there are good hunters and bad hunters. Good people and bad people. And the traits transfer readily and easily to the children.

The way in which we conduct ourselves as hunter-parents is of such serious importance because of the nature of our lifestyle. Hunting is a blood sport. Regardless of how much poetry we write about sunrises and how deeply we appreciate and admire the beaty of nature, the goal of the hunt is to kill. Behind the thin veneer of cultivated civility with which we conduct ourselves in public, and most of the time in private—we are killers.

This responsibility should never be taken lightly, and it should not be lost on us as hunter-parents that we are exposing our children to this during the most vulnerable and formative stage of their lives. Hunting and killing should be conducted with thoughtful purpose, with intent for consumption, and with respect for the life being taken. If we aren't teaching and exemplifying these traits, we aren't raising future hunters, we are raising sociopaths. In rare instances, we as hunters may find ourselves in a moment of callus insensitivity to such matters and realize that our ethical compass needs to be re-calibrated. This has happened to me twice in my life. Once immediately after coming home from the war in Iraq. And once after killing a crow in my own backyard.

My son was five years old in the winter of 2014. He had just recently been promoted from the rank of little boy to hunter apprentice. This was a promotion that occurred intentionally at the age of five, but without fanfare or conferring titles. My wife had drawn this line in the sand before the boy's birth. He could begin tagging along on real hunts at five years old. I had argued against this a little in the early stages of the proposed age restriction, but lost soundly.

Three inches of snow had fallen overnight, and I decided the boy and I should go squirrel hunting. I am not a serious squirrel hunter, but it was a good excuse to get out and walk in the fresh snow. Snow is not exactly rare at this latitude, but it is not frequent either. We normally get two or three winter weather events like this per year, and it will stay on the ground for a few days before melting away with the next warm front. It is also rare enough that schools are cancelled with little more than a dusting on the roads.

I bundled the boy up with layers of clothes until he could barely walk, grabbed the Winchester .22 rifle from the top of the kitchen cabinets, and we headed out the back door. We crossed the back yard and into the ten acre woodlot behind the house.

We walked slowly, watching the trees and listening for squirrels. I stopped to show the boy deer tracks in the snow, which we followed into a thicket and then up a hill and into the neighboring horse pasture. Turning back into the woods to continue the hunt, we followed a shallow draw down to the edge of a thicket. With our backs to the thicket, we sat on a cedar log and watched closely for movement in the trees. We sat for a minute or two before the boy got cold and we decided to continue walking. We stopped again to examine deer tracks in the snow and then followed them to the fence line. It was a boring hunt, squirrel wise. We never saw a single squirrel and began to walk back south toward the house. The boy was tired and asked for a ride. I propped the rifle against an oak tree and lifted him up onto my shoulders. With one hand on the boy's ankles in front of my chest and one hand on the rifle, I continued the walk towards home.

As we walked down the trail leading into the back yard, I saw a crow on the ground by the chicken coop. I stopped and pointed it out to the boy. It was standing in the snow and pecking around at the ground in an area where we often throw out chicken scratch.

"Can we kill it?" he asked.

"Sure," I said, lowering him down slowly to slide off of my shoulders. "Let's see if we can sneak a little closer first."

We eased forward another twenty feet keeping a clump of locust trees between us and the crow. Propping the rifle against one of the locust trees, I settled the iron sights on the crow's head. I could feel the boy's hands on my legs as he stood behind me and peered around the tree. I squeezed the trigger and saw the crow flop about a foot up into the air and then settle lifelessly on the ground. The boy ran out to the bird and stood over it as I walked up behind him.

The crow laid on its back with its wings loosely against its sides. It was inky black and stood out in stunning contrast to the clean white snow on which it laid. There were a few drops of bright red blood on the snow near the bird's head. I picked it up and showed it to the boy, spreading its wings and turning it around in my hands.

"Let's go show Mommy," the boy said.

"No, Mommy doesn't want to see this. Let's just throw it in the woods."

The boy stopped in his tracks and looked up at me as if I had just suggested we burn our own house down. "We can't just throw it away. We have to eat it." The boy's face was serious as the grave.

"Crows aren't good to eat," I said.

"Then why did you kill it?" the boy asked.

I instantly recognized the sharp shift in the pronoun used in the question. It was no longer "we," but "you." Moments before, it was "can we kill it?" Now it was "you."

"Why did you kill it?"

I also recognized the shift in the boy's attitude toward the whole event. I had raised him to understand that we hunt for food and not for sport alone. We eat what we kill. In his mind, this was no longer hunting. What had started out as an innocent squirrel hunt had turned into a crow murder. I was at once proud of his recognition of the difference, as well as ashamed that I had killed the bird at all. The boy held the crow, and I could see the regret on his face. I realized that I was in dangerous territory. This five-year-old child was the most compassionate person that I knew, a trait that must be protected and nurtured. I did not want him to ever become jaded or numb to the act of taking a life—any life.

"You're right buddy. We're going to eat it." I assured him. I had to rectify the situation. Eating the crow would justify the crime and preserve my integrity.

I told the boy to go inside and warm up. I took out a pocket knife and breasted the crow beside the tree line and threw the carcass deep into the woods before the boy could return with any ideas or suggestions of a crow burial or crow funeral. I really did not want to have to dig a hole in the frozen ground or try to write a eulogy.

I brought the meat inside, each breast about twice the size of a dove breast and dark red, almost the color of liver. I rinsed the meat in the sink and washed the blood off my hands. I heated a skillet and cooked the crow breasts whole in butter with salt and pepper, then sliced it thin on a plate. The boy, eager to try it, took the first bite.

"That's gross!" he said. "Let's not shoot anymore crows!"

I took the next bite, and I agreed. It tasted as much like liver as it looked and had a strange grainy texture. It was the nastiest damn bird I had ever tasted. I couldn't believe how bad it was. Surely this bird had been eating roadkill all winter. I have eaten fishy tasting diving ducks and mergansers that tasted better. But I couldn't throw it away, and the boy didn't want any more of it. So, the rest was for me. The boy watched every bite, and I didn't dare suggest throwing it out and wasting the meat after the conversation we had.

So, I sat and ate my crow, both figuratively and literally. I finished every bite, each tasting worse than the last. I placed the empty plate in the sink and retrieved a cold beer from the refrigerator to wash it down. The beer didn't taste good either.

CHAPTER TEN

GUT PILE

The weather man said an "Arctic blast" was on its way, and would reach Central Kentucky just after sunset. I had never heard this term before, but the explanation from the weather man was straightforward with no surprises. A blast of Arctic air from the polar vortex would swoop down, much more southerly than usual, causing a rapid drop in temperatures and unseasonably cold weather. It was like a super cold front. It was a deer hunter's dream come true.

Any hunter will tell you that some of the best hunting, or at least the potential for great hunting, happens around significant weather changes. Duck hunters pray for cold fronts to push ducks south along their migration path. Turkey hunters love to hunt sunny days after storms pass through and the barometric pressure is on the rise because turkeys are likely eager to gobble. Deer hunters will reschedule important meetings or cancel dates with pretty women to be in the tree stand if temperatures drop drastically during daylight hours. This is especially true if it coincides with a full moon or a new moon. Or if the moon is overhead or underfoot. Or if it happens during any part of

November. Honestly though, no serious deer hunter is scheduling any important meetings or any dates with pretty women, or ugly ones for that matter, during the month of November. There are much more important things to do during this time.

The Arctic air was set to hit around sunset, causing temperatures to plummet to nearly 0 degrees overnight. It was late November, and the deer rut was winding down as most of the does had already been bred. Daylight buck activity had diminished over the last several days, but the cold front was hitting with perfect timing. Deer would surely be on the move, feeding – sensing the cold front and snow that would be moving in soon. Deer and other animals are incredibly attuned to nature. They can sense weather changes coming before they arrive. It was also the last weekend of rifle season. Perfect timing.

The boy had never been on a deer hunt up until this point. They are just too boring for a 7-year-old kid. Too much sitting still and quiet, without much of anything going on. Though he had been on a couple fair weather duck hunts, and had been present to see a turkey get called up and killed the past spring. And his love affair with fishing had already begun. But deer hunting had yet to be attempted. I decided that day would be his first, figuring we would go out late, hunt for the last two hours of daylight, and that surely I could keep him engaged for that long. I felt like the potential for seeing deer was high.

We began the normal preparations that accompany taking a 7-year-old child hunting. Dressing in layers, filling a thermos with hot chocolate, gathering snacks, and trying to instill some excitement about the hunt. I didn't have a child-sized orange vest, so I tied an adult vest in a knot in the front to help it stay on his body. Almost as an afterthought, I grabbed the old bolt action .270 rifle on the way out the door.

We left the house at a quarter to four, only about an hour and a half until sunset. We were hunting the neighbor's property, and it was only about a 300-yard walk from the back door. We crossed the yard and had to turn back twice to shoo errant chickens back toward the coop that were trying to follow us. We stopped at the three-strand barbed wire fence that separated my small property from the neighbor's. I propped the rifle against the opposite side of the fence and lifted the boy over. We began walking down the fence line of the horse pasture. The property was twenty-two acres of rolling hills, and about 80 percent pasture, with hardwood draws that fell away into neighboring woodlots. The neighbor kept three horses on the property. As we walked slowly, I explained to the boy that deer have a marvelous sense of smell, and that we'd better try to mask our scent. After saying this, I pointed to the nearest pile of horse dung and stomped on it dramatically. First with my left boot, and then with my right, giving both a good twisting motion. I looked up and smiled. The boy laughed out loud with joy and did the same. He spent the rest of the walk zig-zagging back and forth, stomping on every horse pile within 20 yards of our direct walking path.

"Mom isn't going to like this," he said at one point.

"That's what hunting boots are for. It's okay to get them dirty! But just in case, we don't have to tell Mom".

He stopped to look at me, still smiling, and said, "Oh, I'm telling Mom!"

We arrived at the spot around four o'clock and set up stools in the natural ground blind, which was at the base of an oak tree, had cut cedar branches for cover, and overlooked the back quarter of the pasture. It sat near the top of a narrow, wooded draw— a mix of oak, hickory, and cedar—which fell away to our left and turned into a thicket below us on the neighboring property. The pasture in front of us was kept short by the horses, and there was a small pond in the middle with cedars around the edge. About forty yards behind and uphill from the blind was a three-strand fence at the border of the adjacent property. Perched some fifteen feet up in the oak tree where we sat was a rotted wooden platform from some previous deer hunter, probably fifty years before. I pointed it out to the boy. "It must be a good spot if somebody went through all that trouble to build a stand here a long time ago."

The wind had been blowing all day ahead of the cold front, and as we settled in and poured the hot chocolate from the Thermos, I realized that the wind had completely settled. In the calm and quiet, I could feel the temperature dropping already. I handed the Thermos cup to the boy and told him it was time to get serious and be quiet. The boy sat and sipped his hot chocolate, looked around, kicked his feet, and fidgeted. Just as I was about to whisper-scold him to settle in and be still, I heard heavy hooves galloping uphill from our position toward the fence line. I have had the horses come in and ruin hunts before, and I was already shifting my weight to get up and run them off.

I turned just in time to see a large-bodied buck with tall white antlers jump the fence from the property up the hill and enter the top of the draw, about forty yards from the blind. After jumping the fence, he paused and looked around for a second before walking from right to left along the fence line with his nose to the ground. The boy had turned to watch at the same time I had. "Cover your ears," I whispered, as I raised the rifle to my shoulder. The scope reticle settled behind the buck's front shoulder. A loud shot pierced the quiet of the evening. The buck kicked out his back legs and bolted forward about 20 yards before stopping and standing still, with his tail flicking back and forth. The boy said, "You missed!" and before I could tell him otherwise, the buck staggered to the left and fell, motionless, to the ground.

The boy was ecstatic. He tried to run to the fallen buck, and I had to pull him back into the blind by his vest. I explained that we needed to wait a few minutes to make sure he was dead before approaching, the dangers of approaching a wounded animal, and how to approach safely. After waiting about 10 minutes, we left the blind and walked to the spot where the deer had been standing at the shot. I pointed to the tuft of hairs and the small spatter of blood on the ground, then let the boy lead as we approached, practicing exactly what we had just discussed. He approached slowly, from behind. He walked around wide to get a view of the deer's eyes. He looked at me and said "His eyes are open." He looked around, picked up a stick, and poked the deer's side. "We got him!"

The most memorable and important moments of fatherhood for me have ridden on that little two-letter pronoun. Every time during his childhood that I had killed a turkey, or a deer, or caught a big fish, or completed some task or chore around the house, it was always "we." We did it. Together. "We got him."

The boy's eyes were wild and full of life, excitement, and curiosity. We sat and admired the deer. He was a great buck. A non-typical nine pointer, with a heavy right antler and a skinny left. He had a split left brow tine, and a four inch inside kicker on the right main beam below his G-3. His right antler carried its mass all the way out to the end, with a bladed main beam. He was a beautiful large-bodied buck with a long, old-looking face. Gray hair peppered his snout. None of this mattered, of course. It could have been a spike, and the boy would have been just as happy.

The sun was sinking fast, and the temperature had already dropped noticeably. "We need to get to work," I said, as I pulled a bone handled knife from my belt. I heaved the old buck onto his back and made the first incision on the sternum and began the task of field dressing the deer. I worked quickly and efficiently as I answered a steady stream of questions from the curious boy. After separating everything on the inside of the body cavity, I made the final cut—of the trachea and esophagus, high in the neck—then, with one motion, pulled the entire contents of the body cavity free of the animal and into a large, neat pile. The boy was amazed. He wasted no time picking up a stick and poking around at everything in sight. I pulled the buck away and positioned it on its chest, with the back legs splayed out on the ground to drain the remaining blood from the empty body cavity. The blood cooled and congealed quickly on the cold soil. I called my neighbor to ask if he could bring the tractor out if he wasn't too busy to help get the buck back to the barn. He was happy to oblige.

As the light began to fade and the evening cold began to settle in deeper, I watched steam rising from the fresh gut pile. The curious little boy continued probing at the organs with a stick. I strapped a small headlamp to his forehead for the walk home, then pulled the heart from the pile to show him. The boy was already shaking from the cold, and I rubbed his upper arms and shoulders briskly to warm him as the thick steam from our breath and the heat of the gut pile intermingled, rolled, and danced in the light of the headlamp. We heard the tractor start up in the distance.

***

Kids love a gut pile. Or at least mine does. Every deer he or I have killed since that day, if he is present, gets the gut pile inspection. As soon as the animal is gutted, he hunts up a good solid stick and goes to work. Stomachs and their contents are always of particular interest. He will find the stomach and promptly penetrate it with the stick to expose its partially digested contents. I have had the pleasure of watching the boy conduct this not-so-delicate operation about a dozen times now. Stick selection is important.

I have seen him, on the first couple gut piles, pick up the first available stick and begin poking around. These readily available sticks within arm's reach often prove to be either too small in diameter or too rotted to be good gut sticks. After exploring several gut piles, I watched the boy become more proficient at stick selection. If available, and within close proximity, he seems to favor beech. Beech tree limbs seem to retain their rigidity, and often have a sharp point on the thicker end where they've broken from the tree. After acquiring a suitable stick, he squats by the gut pile and begins separating organs. He looks for the heart first. If intact, we have now; upon his request, begun keeping the hearts to eat. I have never had any interest in organ meat.

Having been raised in the south, you are presented with plenty of opportunities to eat organ meats such as livers, chitlins, gizzards, rocky mountain oysters, and even brains. My grandmother loved to eat pork brains and eggs. The only one of these adventurous dishes that I could partake in was fried chicken livers, which I could tolerate only if each bite consisted of more ketchup than liver. Older folks were much more likely to eat livers and other organs. My grandparents seemed to genuinely enjoy a highly processed lunch meat called "liver loaf" which I have not seen in a supermarket in years. There was also liverwurst, which was eaten on crackers with Tabasco. Later in life,

I gave up fried chicken livers altogether. So, livers, along with other digestive organs, remain "off the table" for my family. We may be barbarians, but we're not savages – or is it the other way around?

Hearts, however, have become a delicacy.

My wife still prefers to scrounge and snack on the night of a deer kill, whereas my son and I will bring home a fresh deer heart for dinner. She is not ready to eat heart, and probably never will be. We usually make heart tacos or heart bulgogi. Both are delicious, and I'm sure there are many other fitting recipes that would be just as good. The key is to slice thin, avoiding all of the chamber walls and cartilage when making your cuts.

After locating the heart and determining if it is still salvageable or if the bullet or broadhead has done too much damage, he goes straight for the stomach. This part of the process is invariably disgusting. It always smells bad, but it is wildly intriguing. He finds the stomach and opens it with the stick.

If the fallen animal was a buck in rut, its stomach is unlikely to have much in the way of contents at all. Bucks in November are much more focused on sniffing out receptive does and so rarely find time to eat, often to the point of malnourishment. But if the deer is a doe, or an early season buck, it is likely to have a full stomach. There is some obvious utility in examining stomach contents for a hunter. What the deer has been eating provides insight into preferred food sources in the area for a particular time of year. We have seen the full spectrum. We have found bucks with stomachs completely empty, as if they hadn't eaten in days. Then there have been doe stomachs so packed full of soybeans and acorns that, when poked with a stick, projected from the organ with enough force to spew out eighteen inches.

The gut pile fascination doesn't stop at deer. We also have to inspect the crop and gizzard of every turkey we kill. After processing the turkey and harvesting all the meat we intend to keep, it is time to investigate. Turkeys, and birds in general, have a different digestive system than us mammals. First, they have a crop—or "craw"—that stores food and begins the digestive process. This will hold food that has been eaten in the last few hours. Next, they have a gizzard. This is a strong muscle, which grinds the food into digestible mush. Turkeys intentionally eat small stones and rocks for grit which remain in the gizzard and aid in this grinding process.

Normal items to find in the crop and gizzard include seeds, grass, clover, acorn pieces, insects, and spiders. Turkeys, being opportunistic predators, will also eat small reptiles, crustaceans, and amphibians. It is always interesting and useful to see what has been on the menu recently. In the last several years, we have also begun cleaning and keeping the gizzard stones. We layer them in a tall, cylindrical flower vase which showcases the variation in types and colors of stones each turkey had been eating for grit. Mountain turkeys often have pale, gravel type rocks, whereas turkeys who frequent creek bottoms often have colorful creek stones. Both seem to have a propensity for eating tiny round fossils.

Gut piles and gizzards have become a part of our post-kill tradition. The boy and I both look forward to it. Call it morbid curiosity. Call it research. Call it gross or weird if you want to. But, it is just the kind of "dirty fun" that kids love and adult hunters never seem to outgrow. Maybe we are savages after all.

CHAPTER ELEVEN

TADPOLES AND TURKEYS

"Truth is, everybody is going to hurt you in the end. You just gotta find the ones worth suffering for."

— Bob Marley

The green digital clock on the radio read 4:45 a.m. as the truck turned onto the gravel forest service road. There was a slight jolt as the tires left the smooth paved surface and met the coarse chert rock, causing the boy to fidget slightly in the back seat. He sighed and re-positioned his head, but never opened his eyes. He had been soundly asleep since leaving the driveway about 45 minutes prior, and the change in the road surface did little to disrupt his peaceful slumber. I glanced at my sleeping child in the rear-view mirror and wondered for a moment what 6-year-old boys dream of.

The gravel popped under the tires as the truck made its way down the winding road. The gravel became thinner and thinner, eventually disappearing and giving way to a narrow, packed dirt road that meandered down the spine of a long ridge system, running from northwest to southeast. The headlights were dirty and dim, and shone lazily on the road about 30 feet ahead. We slowed and turned to park the truck at a brown metal gate. I turned the truck off and sat back in my seat. The sounds of popping gravel and engine noise disappeared and were replaced by the sounds of whip-poor-wills and spring peepers in a nearby pond.

Sitting in the dark for a while, letting the boy sleep, I thought about the walk ahead of us. Mentally mapping out the ridge line and finger ridges that lie ahead of me in the dark, I recalled where I had seen turkeys roost in the past and devised a plan for where we would stop and listen at daybreak. "It would take me about 10 minutes to walk there by myself", I thought. "Probably twice as long with the boy." After subtracting this number from the time remaining before sunrise, I decided it was time to wake the boy and get started.

I opened the door to turn on the dome lights in the truck and let the cool air in. Shaking the boy's leg, I told him to wake up and get ready to go. He rubbed his eyes and looked around, slightly confused. "Let's go buddy, they'll be gobbling soon." He looked around and realized where we were and what we were doing. It took a few minutes to gather snacks and supplies. When we crossed the gate, it was already gray light and we had about a half-mile walk ahead of us. We made our way down the old logging road in the gathering morning light. The chirping of the frogs faded as we walked further from the pond by the gate, and the morning soundscape became dominated by whippoorwills. We squinted in the gray light in an attempt to see the little ground birds. They called loudly on the logging road ahead of us, getting louder and louder as we approached until it sounded as if they were right in front of us. Then they would fall silent until we passed by, for about 20 yards, before resuming their singing. Occasionally, we would see a flutter of movement. A small shadow as they flew off of the trail.

As the whippoorwills began to go off to bed, the singing stopped, and the morning air became much quieter without their song. We stopped walking and listened closely when we heard a barred owl hoot in the distance. Every turkey hunter holds their breath and listens as intently as they can when a barred owl calls, because turkeys often gobble immediately after.

Turkeys often gobble at loud sounds in this way. This is called a "shock gobble". They will gobble at almost anything, if they are in the mood to gobble. I have personally heard them gobble at owls, crows, woodpeckers, geese, dump trucks, thunder, cows, artillery, tanks, shotgun blasts, trains, car horns, barges, and even loud coughs. However—and this will be a controversial statement among other turkey hunters—I do not classify turkeys gobbling at owls as "shock gobbles." When a turkey gobbles at all of these other things, it is likely a shock response, but when he gobbles at an owl, it is something else. Something different.

Some percentage of incredulous readers just closed this book and threw it away. I am willing to accept that. However, if you are of an intelligent disposition, and an open-mind, and are therefore still reading these words, allow me to support my statement. All of the other stimuli that elicit shock gobbles do so with a loud, sharp sound, and the subsequent shock gobble response is instant. A turkey will cut off a woodpecker's high pitched "TEEE TEE TEE TEE TEE TEE" with a gobble before he is finished. He gobbles at the thunder as it is still rumbling. He gobbles at the barge's foghorn while it is still blowing. I wonder how many shotgun blasts are met by turkey gobbles that you never even hear because the report of the shot is still echoing through the mountains? He gobbles at the first note of the loud sound. Instantly.

But, he lets the barred owl finish.

A barred owl's call can vary widely, but the basic and most common pattern is an eight-syllable call that lasts a full six to eight seconds. It is a loud and repetitive "WHO" sound, in a distinct pattern that is often likened to the pattern of saying; "Who cooks for you? Who cooks for y'all…" with a drawn-out trill on the end of "y'all" that fades off. It is a loud call that pierces the early morning air and demands attention. But turkeys don't gobble at the first loud booming "WHO" from the owl. The turkey waits. He listens for 6-8 full seconds while the owl says what he needs to say. Only then, he responds with a gobble. The turkey lets the owl finish. No one knows why, at least not that I am aware of. And I'm not sure many people have ever bothered to notice, or given it much thought. An esteemed and well-respected turkey biologist may write me and call me an idiot, and explain the reason why, and that the reason has been documented and proven since the 1970's – but I doubt it.

It is like they are having a conversation. A dialogue, a polite back-and-forth without interrupting each other. What could they be talking about? What could the birds be saying? Maybe the owl is talking about something he saw the night before. The morning news, as it were. Why does the turkey respond? Perhaps in acknowledgement, or perhaps to argue. It's difficult to ascertain tone and intonation in a turkey gobble, but he sounds angry to me. I guess turkey gobbles always sound angry, though.

But, back to the task at hand. The boy and I made it to the ridge we wanted to listen from, and stopped to listen for turkeys. On this particular morning, the owls were ripping it. It must have been an eventful night before, because they had a lot to say. We held our breath and listened closely after every owl hoot, but there was no response. We waited and listened and hoped—nothing. It was a beautiful, clear morning. The wind was calm. The sunrise was bright. I was convinced that I could hear a mile in every direction from the ridge we were standing on, but sunrise came and went, and no turkey ever gobbled. It happens like that sometimes. All the conditions seem perfect, but all the turkeys in the county silently agreed that they would not gobble that day. It is a mystery how they coordinate their efforts like that, but they do. I think it was because of something the owl said.

We waited there for an hour or so. Listening. Talking. Snacking. Building little stick forts in our makeshift blind. Making a miniature mud man... which is like a snowman, but with clay mud. It is hard to keep a 6-year-old in one place and entertained for long. He soon grew bored, and we decided to walk and call, looking for a gobbler. We began walking slowly down the logging road. Listening and calling every 100 yards. The woods here were a mixed stand of hardwoods and pine. On the high points of the ridge system, the trees were almost exclusively pine. About 300 yards into our walk, we came to the edge of a large, square clear-cut where mature pine trees had been harvested recently. The logging road we were walking on ran along the southern edge of it. We stopped at the corner of the clear cut to call. Just as I took a breath and tightened my abdomen to begin to yelp, I heard, "Daddy! Look at the tadpoles!"

There was a large puddle in the ruts of the logging road that was absolutely black with tadpoles. There were thousands. The puddle was about 12 feet long by 10 inches wide with a lower spot in the middle that flared out into a circular shape about 4 feet across. This was the deepest part and was maybe 6 inches deep. It was obvious that the puddle had once been much larger but had shrunk quickly with the lack of rain. Where the water had receded around its periphery were dozens of dead tadpoles, left to dry on the dirt. I pointed this out to the boy, mentioning that if we didn't get some rain soon the remaining tadpoles weren't going to make it to frog-hood. I regretted these words as soon as I said them. They tasted bad as they left my mouth, and I immediately wished that I could choke them back down. The boy looked up at me, then back down at the puddle full of doomed amphibians. Trying to mitigate the damage I had already done, I mentioned that I thought it was supposed to rain in the next day or two. But it was too late.

About 30 yards off of the road, just inside the tree-line where the pines gave way to hardwoods, there was a small pond. The pond was maybe 30 feet in diameter and perfectly round, with a large cedar tree that had fallen into the middle of it from the far side. There were turtles on the cedar log. The boy, making a quick tactical assessment of the situation, decided that it was his life's sacred mission to save these tadpoles. He began to scoop tadpoles up in his hands and transport them to the pond. Over and over, he knelt down and cupped both hands to gather as many as he could. I commended the boy's good deed and told him he had saved dozens of lives already, that it was probably good enough, and that it was time to get back to the turkey hunt. He didn't hear me. Or couldn't hear me. Or didn't want to hear me. He just kept working away, with the white-hot flame of heroism burning in his eyes. It was clear that we weren't getting back to turkey hunting until every last tadpole was swimming freely in that pond.

I pulled out the half-drank bottle of water from my pocket, chugged the rest, and cut the bottle in half with a pocket knife. The boy knew what I was doing and smiled in approval. He took the bottle from my hand and began scooping with it. Looking around, I found a large cedar tree at the edge of the road and sat against it to watch the boy as he worked tirelessly to save the tadpoles. I remarked that most of them would die anyways, and that the survival rate of tadpoles that make it to adult frog-hood was probably a single digit percentage. I told him there were predators in that pond like fish and turtles and snakes. I even proposed the distinct possibility that frogs will eat their own young. I hypothesized, out loud, that maybe they were better off in the mud puddle. All of my statements were met with silence and dirty looks from the young hero. Thirty-two-year-old turkey hunters and six year old, altruistic, tadpole savers just have different priorities.

"Oh well," I thought. The turkeys weren't gobbling to-day anyway. And the boy was having fun. That's all that matters. I got comfortable under the shade of the cedar tree. I pulled out a diaphragm call, put it in my mouth, and made a series of yelps just for the hell of it. I took the call out of my mouth and traded it for a pinch of snuff. Eager to continue the hunt, I looked at the map on my phone and studied the lay of the land to the southwest and began making a plan for when the boy concluded his "tad-pole-itarian" efforts. I looked up and watched him transfer the tadpole puddle to the pond, 8 ounces at a time. I briefly tried to estimate the volume of the puddle, and how many trips it would take him to accomplish his mission. Then I wondered what he would do about the leftover tadpoles that missed the boat and were left wriggling in the mud.

While pondering the math and logistics of the tadpole rescue operation, a sound caught my attention. I felt it in my chest as much as I heard it with my ears, then realized I had been hearing it for a few seconds before identifying it. It was a turkey drumming, and he was close. I "whisper-yelled" at the boy to come to me. He stopped and turned to look at me, confused. He stood up straight, looking annoyed that I had interrupted his all-important work. "Come here now!" I whispered, as loudly as I possibly could.

As he stood and turned to face me, I saw movement directly behind him. Just over the boy's left shoulder, about 50 yards behind him in the clearcut—the full tail fan of a gobbler crested over a rise in the ground. Almost immediately after I saw its fan, the gobbler stood straight up and turned his bright red head to the side to give us the one-eyed stare they are so famous for, before exploding into flight. He flew up into the tree line and set his wings to glide off of the side of the ridge. He looked like the biggest turkey I'd ever seen - at least 25 pounds if he was an ounce. That he could burst into flight so abruptly from a flat-footed stance seemed to defy the laws of physics. And just like that, he was gone. Into the next county. Gone.

The boy never saw or heard any of this, and he didn't believe me when I told him. He just returned to his rescue mission, blissfully unaware of the opportunity we had just missed. He still doesn't believe me, all these years later. I don't blame him or hold a grudge for costing me the giant turkey in the clearcut that day. But I learned a valuable lesson there, sitting under the shade of that cedar tree. It's the people you love the most that hurt you the most.

CHAPTER TWELVE

A DAY AT THE GAR HOLE

We arrived at the Gar Hole just after sunrise. It was early July, and the conditions were right for this particular spot. The term "gar hole" is used by anglers to describe a body of water that is generally not good for fishing. The term evokes images of hot, stagnant water with gar cruising the shallows and gulping air at the surface, and no game fish to be found. Most of the year, the spot we called the Gar Hole was just that, but heavy rains for the past few days had caused the river to rise and the small slough to be deeper than the usual summer water levels. There was also water flowing through a small spillway in the levee from the impoundment across the road, providing fresh, oxygenated water into the river slough. Clean, flowing water like this in mid-summer was sure to attract fish closer to the bank that would normally be in much deeper water.

It was as nice of a morning as one could hope for in the month of July in the South. Seventy-eight degrees, calm, and humid. The stillness in the air foreshadowing the hot and stagnant day that would unfold as the sun climbed higher in the sky. In a few hours the temperature would be in the mid-nineties.

Cicadas were screaming in the trees overhead as we walked down a dirt path to the right of the spillway and arrived at the edge of the Gar Hole.

The boy's first two casts were perfect. Short, gentle casts just to the edge of the flowing water. The first cast was hit instantly, and the boy reeled in a beautiful 10" shellcracker. The second cast produced identical results except the fish managed to shake the hook out just before reaching the bank. Sensing the boy's disappointment in losing a big fish right by the bank, I said "That's ok buddy. You're doing great." I hooked another red worm on his hook. "Keep doing exactly what you're doing."

The boy casted again. A smooth and gentle cast, ten feet out from the bank and in the edge of the slack water. The line tightened and then ran quickly to the right. The rod bent over, and the boy fought the fish to the shore. Another shellcracker that was at least as big as the first. Three casts, two big fish, and no tangles or snags. I began to think that I might be able to bait the second fishing rod and try to catch one myself.

Then, as nine-year-old kids tend to do when things are going great and the plan is working perfectly, the boy decided to change it up a little bit and try something different. Everything was just going too smoothly, and I suspect this makes kids a little uneasy. A bit uncomfortable. The first three casts were perfect— gentle sidearm casts, straight in front. A perfect display of grace and finesse. The fourth cast, however, should be different. He decided this one should really have some power. Something inside him said, "you should really lean into this one."

I saw him load up the shot before he fired, but I didn't have time to say anything. He held the rod far back behind him. I saw him shift his hips like a heavyweight boxer trying to transfer the full force of his body's kinetic energy into the punch. The rod arced forward violently in a powerful motion that was about halfway between an overhead and a sidearm cast. He released the line from his finger just a little too early sending the bait high in the air and at about a forty-five-degree angle to his right. The line sailed over the only tree limb withing casting range—a sycamore limb extending horizontally over the water at a height of about five feet. The hook and sinker landed in the water on the other side of the limb with the line draped across. As the boy began to reel, I told him to leave it. "Let's see if you hook a fish there. Maybe the weight of a fish on the hook will pull the line out of the tree. If we reel it right now it is probably just going to snag that branch and get tangled."

It didn't take long. A fish hit the worm and ran to the left causing the tree branch to shake. "Okay, now reel it up slow and see if you can reel it over the limb." The boy reeled and a medium sized bluegill emerged from the water and dangled directly under the sycamore branch. As the boy reeled, the fish ascended into the tree. It looked as if the plan might work, but as the fish nearly reached the limb, it flopped and twisted violently and somehow tied itself into a knot around the limb. We could not reel any further, and we could not let out slack to lower the fish.

"Well, that didn't pan out. Let's just break the line so the fish can get back in the water." I took the rod from the boy and reeled so that the line was tight, and the limb was bent in our direction over the water. The line snapped and the tree limb recoiled out and waved back and forth over the water. But there was no splash.

There, dangling ten inches underneath a sycamore limb and two feet over the water was a medium sized bluegill. Hanging from the limb and doomed to die like a morbid Christmas ornament hanging from the tree. The boy was distraught.

"Dad, we have to save him!"

"We can't reach him buddy."

"I'll go get him," the boy said.

I hung my head, knowing what was about to occur. The boy wasn't going to let it go. Killing a fish to eat is fine. Feeding a fish to the turtles that swallowed a hook and might not survive is also acceptable—not ideal, but acceptable. He understands the circle of life. But leaving a fish suspended in the air to suffocate and rot in the summer sun is unacceptable. I also knew the wrath to come when we got home if my wife found out that I let the boy wade out to save this fish.

I sat down and removed my shoes. Wading out about knee deep into the Gar Hole, I grabbed the tree branch and bent it back toward me until I could reach the fish. Holding the branch with my right hand, I grabbed the fish around the body with my left and pulled it free. As I waded back, I removed the hook from the fish's lip and presented it to the boy. He took the fish from my hand and bent down next to the water and released it.

"Why'd you let him go?" I asked.

The boy turned to look up at me and said, "He's been through enough."

I agreed that he had and added, "So have I!"

We continued fishing and joked about the stories that fish would tell about his adventures at the Gar Hole. The boy suggested that maybe he would brag to his friends about beating up the humans and escaping. Maybe he would become a local celebrity and get all the prettiest girl fish.

I provided a darker alternative story. He was now a grizzled veteran who had seen terrible things and lived to tell the tale. Giants who breath without water and hang their enemies from the trees to torture them before deciding their fate. None of the other fish had seen what he had and survived. No one believed him of course. They all called him crazy. Traumatized, he lived out his days in the deep water, too paranoid to eat, wasting away in isolation. A fate worse than death. The boy agreed that I was probably right and that if we were to catch him again, we should just keep him for the fish fry.

CHAPTER THIRTEEN

CONFESSIONS OF A LIAR AND A LARGEMOUTH BASS EATER

Parenting requires most people to develop skills, and even personality traits, that they did not possess prior to becoming a parent. Like it or not, becoming a parent changes you. It has to. The survival of our species depends on it. Take a moment to think back and remember who you were before your first child was born. Think about your personality. Your capacity for serious responsibility. Your priorities. Your values. Think about what you did with your spare time. The people you spent your time with. What time did you go to bed? What time did you wake up? How did you spend your money? Most of us, if we are intellectually honest with ourselves, would reflect on our pre-parenthood selves and say that we were completely different people.

Some of us require more changes and adaptations than others, but there are some traits that could be considered universal requirements for successful parenting. Resilience. Patience. Adaptability. Empathy. Communication. Love. Consistency.

For some, these traits come naturally. For others, it takes work; a conscious effort to be a better person. There are seemingly endless books and resources on the subject that are available to help those new parents who either don't know what they are doing or acknowledge their need for change. There are blogs and podcasts. Magazines. Support groups. All these resources will say basically the same types of things and encourage parents to develop these same universally important traits.

But there is another universal trait that will rarely be talked about in these "better parenting" circles. It will rarely even be mentioned, but it is just as common as the rest of these traits, and just as important. Parenting will make you a liar. No matter how strong you believe your integrity to be, you will find yourself telling lies. Little white lies. Though they're usually harmless, and easy to justify if you have a sensitive moral disposition. But you will lie. Fatherhood will make a liar out of an honest man. And if you were already a liar before becoming a father, like me, your transition will be all the easier.

If you find this pill difficult to swallow, allow me to ease your troubled conscience. It is a necessary evil to preserve some of the magic of childhood, build confidence and creativity, and instill hope for the future. And most of the time, it causes no real harm.

The Easter Bunny.

The Tooth Fairy.

"That's the best drawing I've ever seen!"

"You can be anything you want when you grow up."

"You can do anything you put your mind to."

"Good things happen to good people."

"The cat ran away from home."

Lies.

The drawing sucks. Little Jimmy ain't playing in the NBA when he grows up to be 5 feet 4 inches tall. You probably can't play video games and make TikTok videos for a living, no matter how badly you want to. Bad things happen to everyone, including good people, for no reason at all. And the damn cat that wouldn't stop pissing on the carpet was dropped off next to the dumpster behind the Waffle House. I'm sure he's fine.

There is another lie that I found myself telling my son beginning at about the age of seven. That is the lie of "Fishing Season." For most of his childhood, I told him that fishing season does not open until the last week of May. This is a lie, of course. You can fish year-round. There may be some restrictions on when you can keep certain species, like trout in some areas, or what sections of a certain body of water can be accessed at certain times of the year. But, there is always somewhere to fish and some species of fish to be caught during any season. If a man wanted to, he could fish 365 days a year... 366 in a leap year!

So, I lied.

It may sound selfish, but I had to do it. I had to lie to protect my own interests. No matter how badly the boy wanted to go fishing on a sunny April morning, we couldn't do it. "Sorry, son, fishing season isn't open in April."

At the age of seven, my son had already become a passionate fisherman. Most of the year, I would happily take him fishing any time he wanted. He especially began to get the itch when the weather would warm up in the springtime – like any good angler. This, however, caused a slight problem for me. I am a passionate turkey hunter. In Tennessee, spring turkey season opens the beginning of April, and runs roughly until the third week of May. That is only six weeks out of the fifty-two weeks in a year when I can do the one outdoor activity that I am most passionate about – hunt turkeys. Expressed as a percentage, that is approximately 11% of the calendar year. Therefore, this time is sacred. The other 89% of the year I spend in anticipation. Dreaming of the 11% of the year when I can be in the wild, with a clear purpose, and no anticipation or desire for anything in the future. Completely present. This 11% is mine. More precisely, it is ours. I do not shun my responsibilities as a father during this time. My son turkey hunts with me as much as he wants to go. He killed his first turkey at nine years old, and has become an avid turkey hunter himself. Perhaps a better way to describe it is 11% for turkeys, and 89% for fishing. Surely, 11% doesn't seem like too much to ask, right? My little white lie never hurt anybody.

My conscience is clear.

Fishing season opened the third Monday of May in our family. The day after turkey season ended. That was the lie that we lived. Crappie fisherman will say that we missed the best fishing of the year during that overlap. While I can admit that we certainly sacrificed some good springtime fishing opportunities for my turkey obsession, there is still some great fishing to be done in late May through June. This is when bluegills are on bed, and that is about the most kid friendly fishing there is. That's when we kicked off fishing season every year.

The boy became even more serious about fishing at around age nine or ten, when he decided he wanted to eat our catch. We had spent the first couple years of his fishing career on a catch-and-release program, which I was fine with. I really was not interested in bringing them home and cleaning them. I remember eating crappies when I was a kid, and my grandfather would clean them. I loved it then but had no real interest in going through the hassle of cleaning fish myself. I had cleaned some fish to eat on other occasions, usually while camping, and it was always a messy pain in the ass. It hardly seemed worth it to me when I could just buy catfish filets at the grocery store.

One summer morning, the boy and I were fishing a farm pond where we had permission to do so, and the farmer was insistent that we keep some of the big bluegills we were catching and take them home. I explained that we were just fishing for fun, but he insisted. He told us to bring them to the barn and he would filet them out for us. The boy was excited about the idea, so we kept about 20 big bluegills in a bucket, then took them to the barn. The old farmer pulled out an electric filet knife and plugged it in and went to work. We watched as he expertly fileted the 20 fish in about ten minutes. Maybe five minutes. He was quick, clean, and efficient. He would lay a fish on the table, make a slanted cut with the filet knife right behind the gill, and run the knife horizontally down the spine, stopping just before cutting through the last of the skin by the tail. Then he'd lay the fileted side out, skin-side-down, and run the knife along the skin, separating the meat. It was clean. Graceful even. He made it look so easy. It was like watching art in motion.

We went home and dredged the fillets in cornmeal and fried them for lunch. It was delicious. The boy was hooked. He said it was the best thing he had ever eaten. We went that afternoon to the local sporting goods store and bought an electric filet knife.

During my short career as a history teacher after leaving the Army, I would often discuss important inventions or technological advancements throughout history with my students. We would cover the impact of these advancements within the context of whatever we were studying at the time and why they were considered to be historically significant. Examples included the wheel, the plow, the cotton gin, the printing press, refrigeration, and the light bulb. We also discussed how certain inventions or advancements may have changed the course of history, for better or worse, in the context of warfare. The longbow, for instance, won the Battle of Agincourt during the Hundred Years War. Spanish firearms decimated the Mayan Empire. The atomic bomb brought a swift end to WWII in the Pacific theater.

The electric filet knife was just such an advancement. While our fishing "casualty" numbers surely don't compare to the Spanish conquest of Central and South America, or the destruction wrought by atom bombs in Nagasaki and Hiroshima, the panfish population of Middle Tennessee and Kentucky definitely took a big hit once we learned how to use an electric filet knife. Scholars believe that around 6,400 people were killed in the Battle of Agincourt in 1415 A.D. Roughly 400 English and 6,000 French soldiers. It is not unreasonable to estimate that throughout the boy's childhood we must have eaten more fish than the English number, and in the next few years may approach the French casualty numbers.

If my little boy liked fishing as a "catch-and-release" sport, he loved it once he discovered the delicacy of the Southern fish fry. He became a voracious predator. He wanted to fish all the time, and he wanted to fish for keeps. We had to have discussions about ethical harvest, creel limits, and personal restraint. But, even with these self-imposed restraints, we ate a hell of a lot of fish. Bluegill, shellcracker, catfish, and even bass. We ate them all.

Call me a barbarian, but 15" largemouth bass – fileted and soaked in buttermilk, rolled in yellow cornmeal, and fried in oil—is just as good as any panfish. I am acutely aware that keeping and eating largemouth bass is considered heresy by many serious anglers. Bass fishermen are almost strictly catch-and-release. They fish purely for sport, and it is a great sport. Largemouth bass are a lot of fun to catch. But they are also delicious. When me and the little barbarian go fishing, bass get put on ice in the cooler alongside the more socially acceptable "eating fish."

I know men, personal friends of mine, who will seriously reconsider our friendship based on this confession. I am willing to accept this. I am fully aware of the wrath I risk provoking from serious anglers who may read these words. I welcome it. I embrace it. This is a confession, but it is not an apology.

Pass the tartar sauce. My conscience is clear.

CHAPTER FOURTEEN

COLD FEET

We crossed the brown metal gate in the dark, well over an hour before sunrise. It was a clear night with a billion stars in the sky and a waning crescent moon almost directly overhead that looked like a fingernail. When we stepped out of the truck a few moments before, the night had seemed inky black and impossible to navigate, but my eyes had adjusted quickly. There was just enough illumination from the fingernail moon to see the shape of the two-track dirt road in front of us. After crossing the gate, we stopped briefly to adjust gear and talk about the walk ahead. I carried an old army ruck sack on a metal frame with more gear than I am accustomed to carrying on a turkey hunt. A small stake-out ground blind that was brand new in the packaging, a cylindrical nylon bag with a drawstring. A pair of fold out shooting sticks. Two small, folded seat cushions. A green Stanley thermos of hot chocolate. A variety of snacks. My hunting jacket. The boy's hunting jacket. And, almost as an afterthought, a couple turkey calls and a box of 20 gauge shotgun shells. It was important to be prepared and well-supplied. It was the boy's first turkey hunt; as the hunter and not just a ride-along, and I needed to ensure things went as smoothly as possible.

What we did not have in our inventory of supplies was a flashlight. This was intentional as I hardly ever used a flashlight in the woods, especially on turkey hunts. The boy did not see this as unusual in any way. He had been on several hunts with me already and was no stranger to walking in the dark. He had been conditioned to be unafraid in these situations over the years. After all, he was eight years old—much too old to be scared of the dark.

***

In a particular act of parental cruelty, I had made him occasionally close our chicken coop in the dark. It was one of his chores to close the chicken coop door in the evening after the chickens had gone to roost, which was usually a full half-hour before sunset. On days that we forgot, he would have to traverse the back yard to the coop in the dark, which was about 40 yards away from the house and near to the wood line, close and latch the coop door, and then travel the 40 yards to the back door before the boogey man or sasquatch could snatch him up. Of course he used a flashlight for this task, but I made him do it alone. I would busy myself with dishes or something in the kitchen so I could watch through the window. I assured him that there was nothing in the dark that could hurt him and that everything in the woods around here is much more scared of you. I handed him the flashlight and sent him on his way.

I watched from the kitchen window as the flashlight moved slowly across the back yard toward the chicken coop, scanning in all directions. Then, a brief pause at the chicken coop door to complete the task. Finally, the flashlight hauling ass back to the house, bouncing erratically as the boy evaded the imaginary monsters that he was sure were on his tail. His mother was not happy when she heard of the horrors the boy had endured.

***

We made our way down the dirt road in the dark. The whippoorwills were loud and sometimes sounded so close we thought we might accidentally kick one in the road as we walked. The boy was excited and periodically stopped to ask questions. We had been preparing for this morning for months. He was comfortable shooting his youth model 20 ga shotgun and we had practiced a lot recently with light 2 ¾" dove loads. He was unaware that the 3" TSS shells we were using today were much more potent. I didn't tell him because I didn't want him to be nervous about it. I knew he wouldn't notice the kick anyway when shooting at a turkey.

We walked about a quarter mile down the edge of a long field that had been left fallow for the last year and had overgrown with broomsedge. At the western tip of the field, we entered the woods and slowed our approach. I planned to listen from just inside the tree line. The ridge here extended another 200 yards west into mature oak woods before falling off sharply into a bottom full of old growth beech where two shallow creeks converged. It was a beautiful ridge where I had killed several turkeys in the past. It was the first day of the Tennessee youth weekend and I was confident we would hear a gobbler on this ridge or one of the adjacent ridges. Picking out the widest "two-seater" tree I could make out in the dark, we began setting up. We kicked away the leaves and I staked out the little ground blind. This was necessary because the understory here was clean and, being the last weekend of March, there were no leaves growing on anything yet. The woods still looked like winter—

an endless sea of brown, except for the occasional splash of white flowers on a Bradford pear or dark pink on a redbud tree.

We sat down and I whispered to the boy to explain where we were and where the turkeys might be roosted. I poured a cup of hot chocolate and handed it to him. We were early and it was just barely breaking day in the eastern sky. The stars were still out. I took the owl call from my bag and said to the boy, "Let's see if we can get one to gobble early." Placing the old walnut call to my lips and cupping my hands around the end, I made a classic eight note call of the barred owl. Immediately after I finished the call, a turkey gobbled directly in front of us. It startled us both. It was a loud, explosive gobble that pierced the morning air and echoed down the valley. I could hear the almost mechanical sounding rattle in his throat and feel the gobble in my chest. We were close. Too close. Luckily it was still dark enough that we could make some slow and careful adjustments. I took the hot chocolate from the boy's hands and replaced it with his shotgun. I set up his shooting sticks for support, aimed in the direction of the turkey.

In the minutes that followed, the darkness faded and gave way to the gray light of morning. The turkey began to spit and drum, and I pinpointed his location. He was in a tree forty yards away. I could see him half-strutting on a limb. I tried to get the boy to see him, but he was obstructed from his angle. This was for the best, I thought. "If he can't see the turkey in the tree, the turkey can't see him on the ground." The turkey gobbled again. The boy began to shake.

"Just breathe and stay calm," I whispered.

The boy said, "I'm not shaking because I'm excited. I'm shaking because I'm cold."

It was 36 degrees, and the boy was bundled up like a marshmallow. He had three layers of clothes on, a heavy camo jacket, a toboggan, and gloves.

"How could he be cold?" I thought.

I told him to hang in there and stay ready. I expected the turkey would fly down just under his tree and towards the uphill side. I positioned the boy's barrel in that direction.

The turkey must have gobbled fifty times. With each gobble, the boy's shoulders and arms trembled harder and harder until he was convulsing uncontrollably. I saw the gobbler break strut and adjust his wings against his sides. He dipped his head down and began looking around at the ground below.

"He's about to fly down," I whispered as I turned his safety off. "Your safety is off. Keep your finger off the trigger until you are ready to shoot."

"I'm freezing," he said.

"Oh no," I thought. "His head isn't in the game."

"You can do it Buddy. Just hang in there a little longer and we'll kill this turkey."

I saw the turkey turn on the limb and face the downhill side of the tree, craning his neck around, looking at the ground. He leaned forward and flew down. It was more of a controlled fall, as he landed almost directly under the limb he had jumped from, but slightly downhill from the tree. He made a loud thud as his feet hit the ground. This was a big turkey. As soon as he landed, he flapped his wings and began drumming again. He was in shotgun range, but we couldn't see him because of the terrain. He was directly downhill from us. I made a quick adjustment to the shooting sticks and shifted the barrel facing the turkey.

"Watch for his white head. You're looking for color," I whispered.

I slouched down against the tree to be the same height as the boy. I didn't want to give the turkey an opportunity to see me before he was in the boy's line of sight. "Any second you will see his head coming up the hill," I whispered. Seconds passed. We still couldn't see him. The boy was still shaking. Seconds turned to minutes. The turkey never gobbled, but he was still right there in the same spot. Just downhill. Spitting and drumming constantly. It was the loudest drumming I had ever heard, and I could feel it in my chest. It was hard to distinguish the percussive drumming from my own pounding heartbeat. I tried to point the sound out to the boy, but he couldn't hear it over his own shaking.

"I think he's gone," the boy said in a trembling whisper.

"No, he's not Buddy. He's right there drumming."

"I don't hear anything."

"I promise Bud. He's right there in range. We'll see him any second."

"I'm freezing. My toes hurt so bad."

He was on the verge of tears. I learned a valuable lesson sitting there on that cold March morning. Kids cannot tolerate the cold, at all. A skinny eight-year-old boy cannot generate enough body heat to keep warm, regardless of how many layers they have on. And they cannot see past the discomfort, no matter how exciting or intense the situation may be. The cold is blinding to a child. Debilitating. Nothing else matters but getting warm. Tears were welling up in his eyes and I realized how dangerous the situation was. Not dangerous in a physical sense, but in the sense that he was having a bad experience. I was afraid that this would ruin him, and he would never want to go hunting again. I knew the hunt was over.

I told him, "This turkey is stubborn. I don't think he is ever going to come. Let's just ease up on our knees and see if we can get a shot if he stands still." I knew the turkey wouldn't stand still.

I took the gun and we both got on our knees, keeping our upper bodies low to the ground. I gave him back the gun and told him, "Let's sit up really slow." As we raised up, we came face-to-face with the turkey in half strut. He was standing within an inch of where he had landed twenty minutes before. He saw us at the same time, putted sharply, and ran from left to right quartering away before setting his wings and sailing across the valley. "Oh well," I said. "Let's go walk and warm up."

The boy's mood improved quickly once blood started flowing to his extremities. In a desperate attempt to save the morning, we stopped to play chicken on a large log and flipped some rocks looking for bugs and salamanders. I told the boy that I had some ideas to stay warmer tomorrow. He said "ok" and seemed willing to try it again, which was a relief.

The next morning started out exactly the same except it was three degrees colder. The boy wore the same layered clothes he had on the day before. But today he had handwarmers shoved in every pocket of both his pants and jacket, adhesive toe warmers in his boots, and handwarmers in his gloves. It wasn't enough to merely insulate his body. We needed to generate extra heat.

We returned to the same spot but moved down the ridge about fifty yards. At sunrise we heard at least four different turkeys gobbling. The closest was about 150 yards away and level with us on the same ridge. I heard the turkey fly down and immediately yelped at him. He gobbled back instantly. I positioned the boy's gun on the shooting sticks, and we waited. About two minutes passed and we heard walking in the leaves. The boy was steady as a rock this time. Warm and confident. The gobbler appeared just to the right of the boy's gun barrel at thirty yards in full strut.

"Shoot when you're ready," I said.

"I can't see his head," the boy replied.

"It's the big red thing!" I whispered loudly.

I wondered for a moment if maybe the boy was color-blind. The woods were an endless sea of brown in front of us and the turkey's head was bright red and white. He was in full strut and coming straight toward us. The turkey closed the distance another ten yards, weaving behind trees as he came. I slouched low against the tree and felt exposed. I kept my head tilted downward and peered out from underneath the bill of my hat. The turkey was strutting at twenty yards.

"I see the head now," the boy said.

"Kill him!"

I didn't even hear the shot. But I saw the recoil of the gun barrel and watched the giant gobbler buckle and fall. It looked like he just collapsed under the massive weight of his own body. I grabbed the gun and ran out to the turkey with the boy struggling to catch up. The turkey was stone dead, but soon began to quiver and flop as its nervous system discharged the last of it's energy. The boy watched with utter fascination. He had seen this phenomenon a few times before, but this was the first time it had been induced by his own hand. I gave him time to absorb the moment and watched for his reaction. He was shaking again, but this time from excitement.

When the turkey stopped moving, we positioned him by the tree and packed up the blind. We sat for a while and admired the boy's first turkey; a fine gobbler with 1" spurs and a 10" beard. He seemed heavy, but they all do. We talked and prayed and wondered if he was the same turkey from the day before. We agreed that it probably was, and it felt good to bring some closure to the situation. We stayed there until the boy suggested we start heading home. I wasn't going to be the one to cut this moment short. I sat there with the warm sun shining through the trees and tried to soak in every ounce of the morning that I could. We gathered our things, and I hoisted the boy's turkey over my shoulder as we began the long walk back to the truck. We walked slowly.

CHAPTER FIFTEEN

SUPERSTITIONS

Hunting is an avocation steeped in ritual, laden with ceremony, and often cloaked in mysticism and superstitions. It is highly formalized, with complex sets of rules, and subject to a myriad of regulations and ethical standards; some imposed by state or federal authorities and some of which are self-imposed. There exists a plethora of very specific rituals and traditions that can vary widely depending on the game being hunted, geographical region, subcultures, and even families. Some traditions are deeply personal and shrouded in secrecy, while others are displayed proudly and talked about in broad daylight at picnics and dinner parties.

Hunters and hockey players are the most superstitious people I know. No one else even comes close, except perhaps baseball players. I know this to be true because my son is both; a hunter and a hockey player. A left winger. After observing him and his teammates, as well as professional hockey players, over the last several years it has become clear how deeply superstitious they are. Some players have to be first on the ice. Some have to be the last off the ice. Some will carefully and deliberately step over the blue line while skating during pregame warmups. Some will step on it with both skates. Goalies talk to goal posts and crossbars. Almost every player is particular about the order and process of putting on their gear and taping their stick. And the list goes on. Wayne Gretzky, arguably the best NHL player in history, put baby powder on his stick and drank specific drinks in a specific order between periods. Seemingly, there is no player immune to such superstitions, and to the uninitiated like me, they can seem strange and even a little silly.

Hunting superstitions and rituals are often conducted in private, and rarely admitted to others. But they are just as common. Modern hunters often eat specific foods or drink specific beverages on the day of a hunt, or in celebration of a successful hunt. Lucky hats or shirts are commonplace. I do not consider myself particularly superstitious, but my nightly bourbon changes to Wild Turkey 101 the night before opening day of turkey season and is then the only bourbon drank in my house until the season ends in May. This is not to say I think my luck will run out if I have a glass of Elijah Craig or Jim Beam instead of Wild Turkey... but why chance it?

The Koyukon people of Northern Alaska have kept their hunting rituals focused and standardized through generations upon generations of tribal tradition. In his book, *Make Prayers to the Raven,* Richard K. Nelson shines a light on these traditions for the world to see. A privileged and intimate glimpse into a living anthropology, preserved since the last ice age. The Koyukon rituals surrounding hunting are fascinating and complex. They have very specific rules about how to handle their game animals, who should do so, and how to use the meat, fur, and other products derived from the animals. There are many rules dictating the butchering of animals, including what direction they should face and who should conduct certain tasks. There are many things that women are forbidden to do, touch, or even look at. There are even more taboos for a pregnant woman. For instance, a pregnant woman can't even look at a bear, much less eat the meat.

One fascinating belief held by the Koyukon is that of the collective conscience of an animal species. And in case I am misinterpreting the belief; if not a "collective" conscience, then maybe a "connected" conscience. Or maybe neither. Perhaps it's just a superstition. Whatever they would choose to call it, the Koyukon; as I understand it, believe that if a hunter mishandles or disrespects his quarry, then other members of the species can then begin to sense the presence of the hunter. Game animals can sense or detect his presence and his malicious intentions, and will then avoid him, rendering him ineffective as a hunter. As a result, he carries with him a sort of curse, or a negative energy, or perhaps just becomes unlucky. This could come as the result of mishandling a harvested animal. Or being wasteful in the use of the animal. Or being ungrateful, or boastful, or disrespectful. These things can offend the spirit of the fallen prey and become the catalyst for his bad luck.

A further disclaimer seems appropriate here. It is entirely possible that I am misinterpreting the Koyukon beliefs. Their traditions are varied and complex, and I admit that I am dull and ignorant in comparison to their generations of compound wisdom in such matters. I read Nelson's book and found it enthralling, but I am nowhere close to being an authority on the subject. If I have misspoke, then I offer my sincere apologies to the Koyukon people and Mr Nelson.

A hunting curse is the hunter's worst fear.

We, as hunters, all believe in the curse, at least on some level. We may not admit to our superstitions openly. We may act like sensible and rational people most of the time. But deep down, in the back of our minds. In the dark and cold recesses of our consciousness. In the places we don't bare at picnics and dinner parties. Private places. Quiet places. When we are alone and still and intellectually honest with ourselves – we believe. We believe because we have seen it. A hunting buddy goes on a two-year drought without killing a single deer. Or he misses three turkeys in a row. We believe that it can happen to us, too. So, we take the necessary precautions. We wear the lucky shirt. We say the prayer. We pick up the feather lying in the path in front of us and put it in our hat. We carefully step over the blue line. We do whatever we can to stave off the bad luck. Just in case.

I believe it has happened to me already. I am cursed.

My family and I have been fortunate and blessed for many years with most of our hunting pursuits. We kill enough deer and turkeys to sustain ourselves. We catch plenty of fish in the summer. On the rare occasion that we go squirrel or rabbit hunting, we enjoy modest success. I am always careful to honor and respect the game that I hunt, as well as the wild places that I hunt in – lest I become cursed. And I teach my son to act in the same respectful manner with a solemn and serious tone. A deer or turkey curse would be devastating. Not only would it affect my family's preferred food supply, but it would likely send me on a downward spiral into madness and depression. Thankfully, my curse is of a more minor variety.

I am the world's worst morel mushroom hunter.

The boy and I began foraging for various types of mushrooms several years ago, mostly as an excuse to get into the woods during the offseason and as something fun to do while scouting for deer in the summer. Depending on the season, we have had some modest success. We have found tons of chanterelles in the summer. These are the easiest to find and most abundant. We have found a few chicken-of-the-woods and lion's mane. But, the most prized mushroom of all to most foragers is the morel mushroom.

Morel—of the genus Morchella—describes several different types or varieties including the black morel, yellow morel, and half-free morel. They all look similar, with a round or conical brain-looking cap and a hollow round stem. They appear in the spring of the year when soil temperatures reach 50 degrees, and grow for about three weeks. They grow throughout most of the U.S. and prefer moist but well-drained soil around certain tree species such as ash, elm, poplar, and sycamore. Or so they say.

I spend more time in the woods and walk more miles during the spring of the year than almost anyone alive. I say this with confidence, because morel season coincides perfectly with turkey season. And though I do not claim to be the best turkey hunter in the world, I can confidently claim that I work harder at it than almost anyone. As a matter of fact, if I was a better turkey hunter, perhaps I wouldn't have to walk as many miles! I might not have top tier turkey hunting talent, but make up for it with dedication and determination. When it comes to effort, I have no superiors and damned few peers. I am out there every chance I get. Covering ground. Lots of ground. And I usually scratch out a couple turkeys for my effort. The boy and I often track our mileage during turkey season, when we can remember to do so, and always end up walking well over 100 miles per season. Most of these miles are spent trolling for a gobble; walking and calling

trying to locate a turkey. While we are walking, we are also looking for morels. In the hundreds of miles we have covered in the
last several years, we have only found about ten. I don't understand it. We cover a lot of ground. We know the trees that they
are supposed to grow near. We look for them every spring. Sta-
tistically, I feel like we should find boat loads of them just by
virtue of the amount of terrain that we cover looking for gobbling turkeys. But we don't. The boy has even gone so far as to
change the name from morels to "no-rels." Because we find
none.

My son believes it is a curse. Being a hockey player, he
is far more superstitious than I and so much more apt to jump to
such shadowy and mystic conclusions. But, perhaps he is right.
There is simply no rational explanation, so I am forced to consider the irrational. I have disrespected the collective spirit of the
morel mushroom in the past, and have brought a curse upon myself. Maybe I squashed young morels under my boots at some
point before I started looking for them on some warm spring
morning years ago, walking through a creek bottom trying to
close the distance on a gobbling turkey. My careless eyes focused on the terrain ahead of me, oblivious to the mushroom
patch at my feet, I must have trampled dozens of them. Such
disrespect. So wasteful. And now all morels can sense my presence and my intentions. They hide from me. They can feel me
coming and collectively decide to shrink down or bend over to
hide under the leaf litter on the forest floor.

It feels silly to admit. A grown man believing in such
foolish things as curses or omens or bad luck. Or that the offended collective spirit of an animal, or mushroom, can cause
the species to avoid the hunter. "Believe" is maybe too strong of
a word. I don't really believe in the curse. I am a mostly

reasonable and rational man, after all. I understand that I am likely just bad at mushroom hunting. We all have our talents, and this is just not one of mine. Luckily, I have much more success with the other species that I hunt. I don't really believe in curses, or bad luck, or even good luck. But, when I find a turkey feather lying in the logging road in front of me, I will continue to stop and pick it up and put it in my hat. Just in case.

CHAPTER SIXTEEN

GENERATION GAP

No generation, as a whole, has ever looked upon the one that followed it with envy or with admiration – only contempt and disappointment. The silent generation looked at the baby boomers and shook their heads. They, in turn, watched Generation X grow up and were convinced that they would drive the country into rack and ruin. Gen X came to regard the term "millennials" as synonymous with incompetence and laziness. And now millennials are shaking their heads at Generation Z. Luckily though, each generation always seems to pull through. Somehow, as a species, we always seem to snatch victory from the jaws of defeat. Survival from the jaws of extinction. We always manage to survive, somehow.

But I'm afraid we're right this time. It has finally happened. Generation Z ain't gonna make it. Surely, this is the generation that will wreck it all.

The construct of these generations is an interesting concept. Each generation is regarded as somewhat unique in culture, values, politics, and standards of behavior, though these definitions vary depending on what source you look to, as do their birth year ranges. Having made my entrance into the world in 1983, I am either one of the youngest Gen X members, or one of the founding members of the millennials. I have no preference either way, I'm just thankful I'm not a part of Gen Z.

Another way to unofficially categorize the different generations is by their wars. The silent generation had WWII. The baby boomers had Korea and Vietnam. Gen X had Desert Storm and some other various operations in Eastern Europe and Central America. Millennials had Iraq and Afghanistan. This system of categorization does not follow birth year, but rather service age. The silent generation, for example, was not born during WWII. They were the men and women old enough to go and fight the Nazis. Millennials were not born during the War on Terror. We were the ones who fought Al-Qaeda and the Taliban. Every one of these generations kicked ass, too! In their own ways, and in their own wars.

It's hard to say what causes the correlation between the wars and the generation gap. Perhaps the war forces the generation who fights it to mature quickly, or to more distinctly solidify their values. Or, possibly the collective experience of a war causes a schism between the society who lived through the experience and those who did not. Perhaps it is just a sub-conscious association. Maybe that's the problem with Generation Z. They haven't had their war yet. And I sincerely hope they don't. That is the wish and the dream of every generation – that we fight this war so that our sons and daughters don't have to. But I fear that dream is futile.

It is an unfortunate and detestable condition of human nature. America's sons and daughters will inevitably be drawn into some conflict during this generation. In some dark corner of the world. Where peoples are fighting over gods. Or gold. Or land. Or oil. Or human rights. Or freedom. Or which direction is the proper direction to kneel while praying to the same God. Ridiculous.

But it will happen. And after it does, Gen Z will start to sub-consciously disassociate themselves from the younger kids and babies that are born after the war is over. Because, "you weren't there, man."

Gen Z, iGen, or centennials. There are several names used to describe the new generation. The years can vary depending on where you look, but Gen Z roughly describes those born from the very end of the 1990s to the present day. Actually, academic sites will say that they were born from the late 90's through the 20-teens, but this seems presumptuous. A child born in 2015 would be eight years old at the time of this writing, and so cannot possibly have developed a sense of culture or values for themselves sufficient to define a new generation. This delineation is based on preemptive assumptions. I'm sure this designation of a new generation is based on solid academic research, and I openly admit that I conducted no such research. I am an observer and a thinker, and this is my rant, so you may carefully and gently place that research wherever your imagination may suggest. Everything after the millennials is Gen Z to me.

Generation Z. The oldest of this hopeless generation is presently about 25 years old, and while they still show the trademark characteristics, some of the more disturbing and obnoxious traits are somewhat muted. Prime time Generation Z currently means children through college age adults. Besides the obvious identifier of age, there are tell-tale characteristics to note.

They shuffle through their meaningless existence; hunched over, eyes cast downward. Addicts to a constant flow of shallow entertainment and consumerism. They live in a fake world, inhabited by fake people and fake friends, staring like zombies into a screen all day. Even while walking from place to place, they rarely look up or acknowledge the presence of the other humans around them. They have no situational awareness. They walk down crowded sidewalks, face down, earbuds in, oblivious to their surroundings. I often make it a point to bump into these people in public places and politely say, "Oh, excuse me. I didn't see you."

Surely, if this behavior continues for another million years or so, people will evolve and grow eyes on the top of their heads so that they can see where they are going! Perhaps hair-lines will have to recede back four to five inches in order to accommodate these new eye sockets. They will probably de-velop a strong upper back to support their permanently hunched form, or extra vertebrae in the neck for greater mobility. And I imagine they will have giant thumbs from a million years of scrolling on phones. Future humans will be strange looking crea-tures indeed.

They rarely participate in any sort of meaningful inter-personal communication, opting instead for social media posts which portray a false, manicured, and filtered version of their own lives. They do this for the likes and comments, and the little hits of dopamine they get from the validation from others.

Dopamine – the human body's natural reward hormone. The brain's "feel good" chemical. This is their drug of choice, and it is a powerful one. Though not powerful in the same way that cocaine or heroin is powerful—no one is going to overdose on their own body's dopamine production. Surely though, this dopamine addiction must be one of the causes of the exponential increase in mental health issues like depression, anxiety, and

ADHD in the last two decades. I make this statement completely unfounded on science or research, as I make all of my statements, but I'm sure it checks out.

As a life-long outdoorsman, what concerns me the most is their mass separation from the natural world. Humans are losing their connection to nature, their ancestors, their natural instincts, food, and primal origins. Playing outside is being replaced by video games and cell phones for children. Hunting and fishing are being replaced by golf for adults. This is their idea of outdoor activity, and as close as most adults get to nature.

We are, after all, predators – and we always have been. But most peoples' connection to their food only begins when they peruse the various pre-packaged meats at the grocery store. Young people are losing interest in, and their connection to, the natural world and the circle of life at an alarming rate. The further they drift from their ancestral origins, the worse the problem becomes.

Depressed, anxious, overstimulated. Pale and vitamin D deficient from lack of sunlight. Riddled with insecurities from the proliferation of unrealistic standards of beauty and expectations of reality. With the attention span of a gnat, learning only what can be shown through a 30 second TikTok video. Credulous and gullible. Confused. They are offended by everything and stand for nothing. Slaves to technology. Narcissistic dopamine addicts, living fake lives and posting stories for their fake friends. Dependent on supplements to balance their diets and medications to balance their body chemistry.

Ritalin for the ADHD.

Zoloft for the depression.

Prozac for anxiety.

Pills to sleep.

Energy drinks to stay awake.

Overstimulated little bastards. But all is not lost. There is still a chance for them to come around. I believe they can change and come up into the sunlight with the rest of us millennials, Gen X'ers, and baby boomers and live productive and meaningful lives. They can start by looking up. Making eye contact. Forging personal connections. And, for the love of God, going outside! The chance for them to make a change hasn't passed. But they're going to have to do it soon, before the damage is irreparable. If they don't join us soon, to steal a third-hand quote from Tom Kelly, "They'll be so late to the party that all the fish sammiches will be gone, and all the lovin' spoken for."

My sphere of influence with this generation is very small. I only have one child of my own, but he has been raised in the outdoors. He is a hunter, forager, fisherman, and athlete. He is well-spoken, and functions well in social situations. These last two traits can mostly be credited to his mother. I was 25 years old when my son was born and felt wholly unqualified for the job, as most first-time parents do. I had no idea at the time what challenges the modern world would add to the already considerable task of parenting in the second and third decades of the 21st Century. No one could have imagined. But I had one dominant and overarching goal as a parent. I wanted to raise my son outdoors, to foster survival skills, and instill a deep connection to nature. It has been 14 years now. So far, so good. But this has not been without challenges and obstacles. Some erected by modern society and technology, some by my own ignorance and stubbornness and firm resistance to change.

It's not all bad, though. For all their faults, these kids somehow managed to get pretty good at certain skills. They are great with computers and websites. They are making progress in science, technology, and engineering. They smoke and drink a lot less than my generation. And they seem to have genuine concern for the environment, even though they don't want to be out in it! Who knows, maybe they can do something to save the planet from all the damage that mine and prior generations inflicted. Maybe there is hope.

Someone bring me my Prozac and help me log in to the Wi-Fi.

CHAPTER SEVENTEEN

IRISH GOODBYE

According to the family stories, I must be at least a full quarter Irish from my father's side. It seems like half the folks on that side of the family, and some from my mother's side, came from the Emerald Isle. We all have blue eyes, and my beard grows out red, abruptly changing from dark brown hair to red, right at mid-sideburn. So abruptly, in fact, that ever since I separated from the Army and grew it out, people have been asking if I dye my beard. When I reply that I do not, the follow up question is usually whether or not I dye my hair. That second negative response usually draws incredulous expressions from the faces of those with less refined manners, like children. And deer hunters.

I was also raised to believe that I was at least a quarter German, because no less than two great great grandparents immigrated straight from Germany before the war started. I am also a quarter Cherokee on my father's side, which could clearly be seen in the complexion of my grandmother's skin and her father's skin, as well as his eyes. We were proud of our Native American blood, and my grandparents celebrated this heritage in many ways, although the lineage could never quite be documented or explained. I was told that I was a quarter French because of the surname, Francis. And my grandfather's early genealogy research showed at least a quarter Welsh.

Apparently, genetic inheritance in my family only comes in quarters, and my quarters, if I were to believe all the stories, added up to at least five or six. I have never been good at math, but even I know that something can only be comprised of four quarters. Any additional quarters just won't fit into the whole of the thing. And since I have not seen any French or Cherokee or German overflowing from my body and leaking out onto the floor, I am apt to believe I am only 100% human, and no more. The math just don't add up.

Around 2013, when the mail-in genetic testing kits became popular and affordable, a few people in my family, including myself, decided to participate. Let me pause here and say that if you are proud of your lineage and have any deep-seated traditions or cultural beliefs because of your background, perhaps it's best to just leave genetic testing alone. You can marry into a family and adopt their traditions without having the blood pumping in your veins. You can also honor and celebrate a culture even if your grandparents didn't come from its country of origin, within reason. But if you are of a curious nature and have an open mind; if you are a truth seeker – take the test. For the edification of the family – take the test. It is illuminating. But be warned, it might not show what you expect.

I won't bore you with the finer points of my genetic make-up, but my test results showed that two of my quarters turned out to be 0%, and another one of my quarters was more like a dime. The family stories were a little off the mark! Other family members' tests had corroborating results.

Some people who get unexpected results just refuse to accept them. They'll throw away the papers and continue to believe the second and third hand family stories over the genetic science. That's fine, and there is no real harm done. A little mild and good-natured cultural appropriation never hurt anyone.

That quarter I mentioned that turned out to be a dime was my Irish blood. It turns out, I am only about 10% Irish. But that is just enough. I can incorporate 10% Irish traits into my personality without feeling pretentious or fake about it. I figure that about 8% is already used up by my red beard and drinking habits! That leaves me with a spare 2% to use on one of the greatest gifts the Irish have given unto the world. That *we* have given to the world. And it is as much a part of me as my red beard and blue eyes – the "Irish Goodbye."

If you are unfamiliar with the term, or you are merely an Englishman, allow me to rend the veil. An "Irish Goodbye" is when you leave a party, event, or social gathering without telling anyone. No thanking the host. No making follow-up plans. No awkward hugs or handshakes or empty promises to "do this again sometime soon." Nope. You just leave. Quietly, unapologetically, discreetly, and whenever the hell you want to. It is a beautiful thing.

Being the anti-social troglodyte that I am, mastery of this skill has changed my life. It can work for you, too – if you're at least part Irish. But if you are unfortunate enough to have no Irish blood pumping in your veins, don't appropriate my Peoples' goodbye. Enjoy the rest of the party.

Having contributed half of the genes to my son's genetic makeup, my Irish dime becomes his nickel, and he is left with 5% Irish DNA. He doesn't have any visibly Irish traits. He has dark hair, dark eyes, and so far, does not even like the taste of

beer. It seems that he has used his whole 5% on the Irish Goodbye, because he appears to have mastered the skill at an early
age.

It happened at about age thirteen, as I'm told it does for
most young people. There was no ceremony or fanfare. No pomp
and circumstance. No announcement or public address. I knew
it was coming long before. I knew because it was the same when
I was a boy, but I didn't want to accept it. At the age of thirteen,
he chose to go to a Halloween party at a friend's house instead
of spending it with the family. Our family has always made a big
deal out of holidays, and not just the major ones. We try to find
excuses for celebrations, just to have good family fun. The boy
had outgrown trick-or-treating a year or two before, but we still
had a family party at home on Halloween each year. We deco-
rated, ate fun snacks, and watched scary movies. But that year,
at age thirteen, he chose to go to a party at a friend's house instead.

"Fine by me," I thought. October 31st is one of the best
deer hunting days of the season. The pre-rut is in full swing, and
mature bucks are hitting scrapes hard in search of the first receptive does of the rut. I couldn't wait to hit the woods.

I spent the evening in a lock-on stand, eighteen feet up a
gnarly looking maple tree. It was in a perfect pinch point at the
bottom of a finger ridge, with a dense thicket to my left and a
deep creek to my right. A heavy trail came out of the thicket
toward the creek and made an abrupt turn southward past my
stand and parallel to the creek bank. Fifteen yards from the base
of my tree, and in line with the southernmost bend of the creek
bank was a large scrape beneath an overhanging beech tree limb.
The wind was perfect; blowing steadily from the west, quartering from the thicket toward my stand, and slightly right to left.

I sat in my stand all evening, waiting and watching. Patient and alert. In the perfect spot, on one of the best days of the year. And I saw nothing. It was the most boring damn deer hunt I had ever been on. I don't even think I saw a squirrel or a bird the whole damn time. It was as if the entire world had abandoned me in this corner of the earth alone. As the evening waned, the still silence left me with too much time alone with my thoughts. I reflected on past Halloween nights spent with my son. I came to the realization that this first Halloween spent without him was not the beginning of his disassociation with his childhood. It had been going on for a while now, but I hadn't really noticed. He was spending more and more time with friends and away from home. When he was home, he was often talking to friends on the phone or playing video games. He seemed less like my little boy, and more like a teenager. I couldn't put my finger on the moment it happened, but at some point in the past year or so, he had quietly and gently slipped away a little bit. He didn't even say goodbye as he went.

I sat there, in the gathering darkness, feeling a bitter sense of loss sink in. I knew that we would likely never spend another Halloween night together. I wondered how many other "last times" had already occurred, without announcement or proclamation. A cool breeze swept across my face and brought me back into the present moment. I continued to sit there long after it was too dark to be bow hunting. As I began to climb down from my treestand, a barred owl hooted close by. I stopped to listen. He hooted again. Another owl answered in the distance. I stood there, at the bottom of the tree in the dark, and listened intently to their conversation. It made me think of turkey hunting, and I couldn't help but smile. The boy loves turkey hunting. I realized then how lucky I was to share that love for hunting and fishing. The closer of the two owls called again, as if to reaffirm his point. Like a reminder from an old friend. "I can't wait for spring," I thought.

All children grow up and find their independence, and in so doing must drift further away from their parents. It's just the natural progression of things. But I can take solace in the fact that he and I have something in common that will always draw us closer together. A common bond that, God willing, will endure for the rest of my life. I know that every available morning this April, my son and I will be together, standing on some oak ridge or logging road and listening for a turkey to gobble. I also know that on clear June mornings, we will be loading up to go fishing. It might not happen as often as it did when he was eleven, but we will still have plenty of time together. We will always have these moments in the wild, free from the pull of distraction and weight of worldly worries. I felt sorry for fathers who don't have this in common with their children, and wondered how they managed to stave off the loneliness when darkness descends on late October evenings like this one.

I made it back to the truck in the dark. Alone, but feeling a little less lonely. Back down in the holler, the owls were still calling and laughing back and forth. I was thankful for the reminder they had given me. Their calls became louder and more enthusiastic. Just to the north of the owls, on the ridge above the thicket, a coyote began to howl. The holler that had been dead all evening was suddenly lively. "It's like a party down there," I said out loud, as I loaded my gear into the truck. I left the party without saying goodbye.

CHAPTER EIGHTEEN

A SEASON IN THE SYCAMORES

Growing up in East Tennessee, my fishing experience was mostly limited to crappie fishing. My great grandfather, when he was still able, would occasionally take me crappie fishing on the Tennessee River. I now understand, many years later, why we targeted crappie when I was a kid instead of going Bass fishing. Vertical jigging from a boat for crappie is about the easiest type of fishing for a kid to participate in. There is no casting involved. You simply flip the bell of the reel and let your bait sink. We generally used lead-head jigs, with live minnows or worms, and dropped straight to the bottom. We would then reel up a little bit, jigging up and down until we got a bite. No casting reduces the number of tangles and knots for a child. Come to think of it, we always fished in deeper water by the dam or bridge pillars where there were less branches and chances for underwater snags. This made for a much less frustrating experience for everyone on the boat.

My great grandfather, God rest his soul, deeply loved taking me fishing with him. But he was much too old, and slightly too drunk, to deal with the headache of a whole lot of snags and tangles from an eight-year-old kid. He wanted to sit back and watch and enjoy. He was content to drink his Budweiser, bait hooks, and put fish in the live-well. He would sit shirtless, on the swivel chair on the bow of the boat, and work the trolling motor and deliver instructions as I fished. I realize now that he was soaking it all in – the sun, the water, the time with his young grandson. He was absolutely savoring every minute of what he realized were his last capable years of life.

I was lucky enough to have fourteen years on Earth with the old man. Me, in the early spring of my life, and he in the waning winter of his. I was probably only nine years old the last time we went on one of these crappie trips together, but if I close my eyes and try, I can still smell the aroma of a summer afternoon at the cleaning table in the backyard. Sometimes, the old man would drink Clamato juice with his beer. Clamato—I'm not even sure it's still in production—was a mixture of clam juice and tomato juice that was popular with old men when I was a child in the 1980's. The pungent aroma of Clamato, Budweiser, and fish guts lingers in my memory like an old friend. The smell is as strong now as it was 35 years ago.

After the old man's passing, I did not go fishing, at least not seriously, for many years. It was just never of great interest. I spent my high school, college, and early Army days chasing ducks and deer and women. I was much more of a hunter than an angler.

In the summer of 2008, I found the right woman. We fell in love, and wasted very little time before starting a family together. Life happened in the blink of an eye, and all of a sudden

I woke up one morning and had a hunting buddy for life. My son. My wife let him start tagging along with me on serious hunts when he was 5 years old. His inaugural hunt was a duck hunt, but after that, his specialty quickly became turkeys. Turkey hunting is great for young kids. While you don't stand a hell of a good chance of killing a turkey when you're toting a 5 or 6 year old kid with you, it is a hell of a good time. Turkey hunting is exciting. On a calm, high pressure April morning, if the turkeys are gobbling, that's enough. Just to hear a gobbler in relatively close proximity is thrilling for a child. There are turkeys and owls and snakes and turtles and logs and creeks and rocks to flip. It is an absolutely fascinating experience for a little boy.

On one such hunt in Tennessee, the boy had been excited by the turkeys gobbling on the roost until they flew down. That morning when they flew down, they stopped gobbling, as turkeys often do. The boy promptly got bored and fell asleep, giving me the opportunity to do some serious calling and maybe draw a bird in close enough for a shot. And that's exactly what happened. After 30 minutes of silence, I saw the full fan of a gobbler crest the ridge. As soon as I saw the fan, I also saw the bird's bright red head stick straight up. His head was colorful and stood out in stark contrast against the drab, brown surroundings. The top of his head was snow white, and his waddles so red he looked like his throat had been cut and he was bleeding out on the forest floor. He would go into strut and then deflate and stick his head up for a good look around, and then spit and drum as he went back into strut. He was performing this dance in about three second intervals. Three seconds of strut, three of standing tall, as he inched his way toward the crest of the ridge. I wished the boy was awake to see it, but there was no time and no way to wake him without motion sufficient to have sent the turkey off the side of the ridge in an instant. I took aim and sent a load of lead #6s through the morning air. The boy jolted awake as I ran out to the bird to make sure he didn't flop down the steep ridge side. We celebrated together. We admired the turkey's feathers and beard and spurs. We prayed. We thanked God, and we thanked the turkey. We talked about the seriousness of the situation. The boy asked a million questions about life and death and feathers and the bird's head and why it flopped around so much after it was dead. We met up with my father, the boy's grandfather, and walked back to the truck. We stopped along the way to play chicken on logs and to scoop up tadpoles in mud puddles and to flip rocks to look for salamanders. It was a perfect morning if I've ever had one on this Earth.

We left the woods and drove to a nearby boat ramp to park and clean the turkey. This was where the serious business of the day began. I had brought along a fishing rod for just such an occasion. The boy and his grandfather started flipping rocks and looking for worms. I began to process the turkey. Soon I heard my son yelling, "Daddy!"

I took a break from plucking the turkey on the tailgate and walked over to where my father and my son were standing on the bank about 40 yards from the boat ramp. The boy had caught a handsome, two-pound largemouth bass on the first cast. He was as proud as if he had just graduated college. He held the fish for pictures and posed and smiled and asked a million questions again. "Why is the fish's mouth so big? Did we hurt it when we caught it? Why is it slimy?" And, of course, "can we do it again?" He caught about a dozen more fish—bluegill and small bass—and loved every minute of it. We hunted the next morning with no success and went home. But, he had found his new passion – fishing.

And thus began our season in the sycamores.

Happy that my son had loved the experience so much, I began looking for local places to fish. I had not been fishing in years, and did not know of many places close to home. I found a small lake, about twenty minutes from the house, where we could fish from the bank. It was more of a large pond, really. It was early May, and the bluegill were "on bed". I honestly had no idea what that phrase meant at the time, but I do now. Bedding season is when fish breed. They group together and make clusters of nests in the sand and gravel in the shallows. They make a honey-comb pattern of circular depressions in the bottom, with a fish guarding each one of the nests. They are easy to spot if you know what you're looking for. It makes for damned easy fishing. As a general rule, the full moon of May is the right time to be fishing bluegill beds. We found one such cluster of beds on our first trip, and caught 30 fish in as many minutes.

When I say "we," I mean "he." He caught 30 fish in as many minutes. Maybe 30 fish in half as many minutes. I was merely the designated tie-er and unhook-er. The fish taker-off-er. The assistant. It was exhausting. It was frustrating. It was a hell of a lot of fun!

It was about the busiest I've ever been. I instructed and mentored. I tied hooks and unhooked fish. I gave advice and untangled lines. I casted for the boy and handed him the rod quickly so he could fight the fish to the bank. He insisted a few times that he should cast himself, but his attempts usually landed the line in a tree branch above the water. I broke lines and retied hooks. We had a hell of a time. We released all of the fish as we caught them. We went home tired and happy, and eager to do it all over again at the earliest opportunity.

The next weekend, we were at it again. And the next weekend, and the next, and the next. We visited every pond I could find. The boy was a child obsessed, and he was having the time of his life. But it wasn't all beer and skittles. It was hard work. The more the boy fished, the more of an "expert" he became. The more independent he wanted to be. He wanted to cast himself. He wanted to pick the spot and choose the bait. He didn't want to bait hooks, though. He left that part to me. The more independent he became, the more my workload increased. With every independent cast came the distinct likelihood of disaster. We discovered quickly, as he became more confident in his casting abilities, that there was a proliferation of sycamore trees overhanging the banks that we fished from. These overhanging branches proved to be formidable obstacles to the boy's casting. He absolutely littered the trees with hooks and sinkers and bobbers. I learned quickly that sycamore trees do not give these things back.

We spent a season there, on the banks of the rivers, lakes, and creeks of Middle Tennessee. Under the shade of the sycamore trees, and often tangled in their branches. We fished as often as our schedules and the weather would allow. We boated. We kayaked. We hiked and we waded. We caught countless fish. I tied countless knots. We made countless memories. We loved every minute of it.

It's one of the peculiar realities of life that you can never truly come to understand another person's perspective. We may think we do. We try to empathize and understand. But we never really know how the world looks and sounds and smells and feels to another person. I often wonder what this season felt like to my son. I hope that he remembers it as fondly as I do. I hope the colors were just as vivid and the air just as sweet.

We spent a season there together, under the sycamores. A long season—not in the calendar sense of the word, but a season of our lives. The boy in the early spring of his life, me in the mid-summer of mine. The boy, learning to fish. The man, learning to be a father. Our season in the sycamores lasted for several years but seemingly passed in the blink of an eye. The days pass slow, but the years go fast.

The boy is now still in the fully bloomed spring of his life. Growing. Learning. Nurturing the seeds of love and hope and strength and knowledge and faith. He is eager and full of life. I hope that he spends all of his seasons well, and that the rest of his spring overflows with sunshine and laughter. I hope that his summer is everything he wants it to be, warm and vibrant, and that he enjoys it as deeply as I have enjoyed mine. And while I do not believe I have yet reached the autumn of my life, I have begun to notice a heavy dew on the grass in the mornings when I wake up. The temperature is just a little cooler at night. I have seen flocks of starlings congregating lately, on still and quiet afternoons. And the leaves on the sycamore trees have recently turned a paler shade of green.

AFTERWORD

In an increasingly synthetic world, people from all walks of life are seeking out the organic. Organic foods, experiences, and ways to connect with nature that are so sorely missing from their day-to-day lives. This has led to an influx of newcomers to the outdoor sports of hunting, fishing, and foraging. More often than not, these newcomers are young families who see the disconnection of the modern world from nature, and desire a better way for their children. They desire something real; longing for authentic experiences in the natural world.

A Season in the Sycamores was never meant to be a "how-to" book on parenting or hunting or fishing. There are no step-by-step instructions or graphics about the proper age to participate in different activities. Every child is different. As is every family. Geographic regions are different. Any attempt at instruction would therefore become too generic. Instead, Sycamores focuses on common themes that all parents will experience when attempting to raise an outdoor child: frustration, patience, determination, adaptability, and a lot of humor. These themes will be part of the experience, whether you are a seasoned outdoorsman or a clueless beginner. Whether you are instructing a child from a position of expertise, or learning a new skill alongside them. Whether you are squirrel hunting in the

Georgia hills, trout fishing in the cold rivers of Montana, or chasing turkeys in the East Kentucky mountains, you will have similar experiences.

Those of us who are willing to rise to the challenge and take a child into the wild in search of adventure and food should understand the importance of shouldering this responsibility. The percentage of hunters and anglers in America continues to decline. Urbanization, habitat loss, and changing societal values all threaten to snuff out a way of life that has been central to the American story for hundreds of generations. There are those who actively seek to take hunting, trapping, and fishing rights from us, and it is our responsibility as sportsmen to represent our community well, to remain educated, and to be politically active to protect our rights. There is another threat to our lifestyle that is just as dangerous; people are losing interest in nature. There are too many distractions in the world today, with the rapid and relentless march of technological advancement, social media, sports, games, and endless on-demand entertainment options. We have become overstimulated and distracted, and children are the most susceptible to these vices.

If we, as sportsmen, hope to protect our way of life and to preserve wildlife and wild places, we must get our children involved in outdoor pursuits. Not just casually, but consistently and radically. We need them to fall in love with nature. We need passionate outdoorspeople of the next generation to carry the torch. To fight for our rights and protect our wildlife and wildlands when we are no longer able. Our children are our only hope, but they need our help. They need our spark. They need guidance and direction. It will take dedication from those of us who are willing. Those of us willing to tie a thousand knots and untangle a thousand tangles. Those of us willing to walk at a child's pace when we want to be running. Those of us willing to get dirty or wet and laugh about it. Those of us willing to coach and teach and mentor with patience and love through their formative and vulnerable years. We who are willing to spend a season in the sycamores.

ABOUT THE AUTHOR

Steven Francis is a passionate outdoorsman, U.S. Army combat veteran, former teacher, writer, and most importantly a father. Born and raised in East Tennessee; he is a life-long hunter and fisherman with a deep personal connection to nature and a passion for wildlife conservation and wildlands preservation. He holds a BS in Political Science and a MA in Education. He currently resides in Kentucky with his wife and son.

Made in the USA
Columbia, SC
04 May 2025